Praise for *28 Voices*

"Not gonna lie, some of these short stories really got to me. They're worth checking, just prepare yourself." - **Paul Hoon**

"Some of these stories are difficult to get through due to the nature of the stories, but overall the anthology was a good read." - **Jake Jacob**

"Written by ordinary people leading ordinary lives. How very relatable it is. I was enthralled by the talent that was gathered together to contribute to this book. I enjoyed it completely and I strongly recommend it." - **Shannon Brennan**

"The writing is honest and heartfelt, and I found myself deeply connecting with many of the stories. This book is a reminder that we are all connected through shared experiences, and that even in our darkest moments, there is always hope and resilience. It's a beautiful testament to the human spirit!" - **Ryleigh Jones**

"This collection of essays resonated with me on a personal level. Each author's voice felt genuine and their experiences, though diverse, were relatable in their own way." - **Alice Garcia**

"Short story collections aren't my usual pick, but I'm so glad I picked this up. Its charm is in how relatable and heartfelt it is. Each story resonates deeply, inviting you to empathize and connect. The talent in this collection is truly impressive. I thoroughly enjoyed it and recommend it!" – **Summer Cole**

RECOGNITION FOR 28 VOICES

The 2025 Central New York Book Awards: Finalist for Non-fiction

BY APPLE AN

Fiction
Mother of Red Mountains
Daughter of Blue City

Memoir
Las Crosses

Nonfiction Anthology
28 Voices
37 More Voices

Nonfiction Self-Help
All-in-One Dotted Journal Notebook

BY GEORGIA A. POPOFF

Poetry

Living with Haints

Psychometry

Psalter: The Agnostic's Book of Common Curiosities

The Doom Weaver

Coaxing Nectar from Longing

Nonfiction

*The Whiskey of Our Discontent: Gwendolyn Brooks as Conscience &
Change Agent*

*Our Difficult Sunlight: A Guide to Poetry, Literacy, & Social Justice
in Classroom & Community*

Anthology

28 Voices

37 More Voices

Voices in Verse

28 VOICES

VOICES HEARD ANTHOLOGY SERIES
VOL. 1

Edited and
with an Introduction by
Apple An & Georgia A. Popoff

Foreword by
Phil Memmer

Voices Heard Publishing, LLC

DEDICATION

To my writing instructors, fellow writers, and many inspiring authors.
– Apple An

To all the writers of the Writers Voice community, and especially the Flowbies and DWC PRO students over the years.
– Georgia A. Popoff

Acknowledgements

We thank Phil Memmer for building an opportunity for the YMCA of Central NY's Writers Voice / Downtown Writers Center (DWC) community to coalesce, where we learn with and from each other, and for all the ways he has supported the literary community since 2001, as well as for writing the foreword to show his support of this project and its participants.

We are grateful that Gwenlyn Davis and Sarah Mawhorter contributed countless hours to review the manuscripts within a tight timeline. We heard from many authors who appreciated the feedback and suggestions that shaped their final submissions.

We thank Susan Keeter's effort and appreciate her artistic talent in turning Kevin Morrow's beautiful photograph into an amazing cover for the volume.

Finally, we thank the contributors who made this volume happen! We appreciate their timely responses on various tasks and the quality of the final submissions.

CONTENTS

FOREWORD

PHIL MEMMER

When the newly created Arts Branch of the YMCA of Central New York opened the Downtown Writers Center (now the Writers Voice of CNY) in 2001, we did so in response to a surprising gap in the local arts environment: there simply was no place in town, at that time, for aspiring writers to take workshops, and no consistent community-based reading series for poets and authors. For a town the size of Syracuse—a town with a vibrant literary history, no less—that felt like a need worth addressing.

Twenty four years later, holding this collection of nonfiction pieces by regular Writers Voice students in my hands, it is humbling to see how far everyone has come—the program, the faculty, and of course the students most of all. After all, for our first few of years, the Downtown Writers Center didn't have much success with nonfiction classes. (Here's a... well, a Wild bit of DWC history: one of the first nonfiction workshops we offered was to be taught by a promising Syracuse University MFA student named Cheryl Strayed—yes, that Cheryl Strayed. Only two people registered, and we were forced to cancel the class.)

These days, nonfiction is one of our most successful genres at the Writers Voice, and our students have had successes of their own—they've written books, been published in literary journals (including our own Stone Canoe), and had their work included in the pages of this new collection, 28 Voices: A Nonfiction Anthology Vol. 1. I particularly love that last bit, as it hints at more to come—new works by current students, as well as new works by those who haven't yet discovered our literary community at the Y.

This first 28 Voices includes stories by so many terrific people that I've had the pleasure of knowing through their years at the Writers Voice. Several of them took their earliest steps as writers at the Y... they took their first class on a whim or at the recommendation of a friend, and (as so often happens) fell in love with the magic of putting words on a page. Then, not content with that initial feeling of wonder and pleasure, they stuck with it and did the hard, necessary work. Apple and Georgia have done a terrific job of collecting some of that work here, and I hope that you'll enjoy every last bit of it.

INTRODUCTION

APPLE AN & GEORGIA A. POPOFF

The YMCA of Central NY's Writers Voice opened its doors in 2001 to offer writing classes in all genres at its Downtown Writers Center (DWC) as the region's only literary center.

As someone who has taken various classes at DWC since 2017, Apple An can attest that she has benefited tremendously. First and foremost, the instructors opened the door to creative writing for Apple and provided much-needed advice. They have been patient, encouraging, and insightful. They ensured trusting environments where attendees, most of them felt vulnerable when started, felt safe, encouraged, and overall, emotionally supported. The fellow writers functioned as a sounding board with constructive feedback and suggestions. They held each other accountable and committed to finding time to write or critique from their busy daily routines. Their writings presented a variety of strengths and styles that were worth learning.

Over the years, these classes helped Apple produce two published short pieces, her debut book, *Las Crosses*, and many vignettes that will be included in her upcoming books. Published in 2023, *Las Crosses* was selected as the finalist for the 2023 Annual Intendent Author Network (IAN) Books of the Year Award in the categories of women's non-fiction and multiple-cultural non-fiction. It also received the 2023 Outstanding Creator Award in the categories of Biographies/Autobiographies/Memoires (3rd place), Travel (3rd place), and Multicultural/Bilingual Books (2nd place).

Most importantly, the people in these classes inspired Apple to form a broader and higher writing goal: to enrich Asian American cultural heritage and history and to enhance cultural understanding and acceptance among all people.

From the DWC classes and several local author events, Apple realized that if we listen to or get to know people, we will find that everyone owns something that can be inspiring—maybe not the same thing to the same people, but there will always be something for someone. Apple also noticed that the majority of fellow writers of DWC classes were interested in sharing their work with a wider audience. Finding an outlet became a perennial topic. Some of them tried and succeeded; some of them either didn't try due to the fear of rejection or failed to land a place.

Apple wanted to find a way to pay back the benefit of DWC services she received and to support fellow authors with an outlet to let people tell their stories and voice their views. An animated brainstorm between Apple and Georgia Popoff, a DWC instructor since its beginning and program director since 2011, took Apple's desire to provide an opportunity to her DWC colleagues, yielding the idea of The Voices Heard Series.

For this first volume, we focused on involving seasoned authors who have been attending programs and classes offered by the DWC. After sending out a call for participation to 109 people in November 2023, we received responses from 37 authors with temporary titles and themes. Subsequently, 31 of them offered first submissions. These manuscripts were carefully reviewed and given constructive feedback from the two editors and two volunteering reviewers,

Gwenlyn Davis and Sarah Mawhorter, resulting in the 28 final essays included in this volume.

These writings recount a wide range of life's journeys and what we've learned from them: childhood memories, life-changing events, love and relationships, childbirth and parenthood, balancing family and career, adapting to new environments or cultures, coping with losses of loved ones, and spirituality.

As editors, we hope this first volume inspires more people to write, write more, and build long-term writing and publishing plans. We encourage all writers to pay forward, to be generous with their time and effort, and to promote each other's work whenever possible. In this literary world, a rising tide raises all boats.

1

THE CHIFFOROBE (PART 1)

JEAN ANN

Invented in the early 1900s, a chifforobe is the size and shape of a dresser, but along with drawers, it has a small closet. The word chifforobe, like the thing itself, is one entity made up of two adjoined but discrete parts. The French word chiffonier, meaning chest of drawers, and the English word wardrobe, meaning closet, are each shortened. Then, the shortened forms are put together to yield chifforobe. This is Part 1 of the story of a chifforobe that has been in the same family for nearly 80 years.

It was 1946. Jean and Tom Savoca had been happily married for twenty years. From their beginnings as children of Sicilian immigrants, they'd worked their way into the middle class. Jean and Tom worked in the garment district of New York City. As a very young woman, Jean had worked as a seamstress. Tom worked as a cutter for a tailor; rarely, if ever, missing a day of work. Once their children came along, Jean had stayed at home to raise them. Now, their daughter and son were about to begin lives of their own; Marian, 18 years old, soon off to Queens College, and Tommy, 14, just beginning high school. But there was a surprise in store for Jean and Tom Savoca: one day Jean discovered that she was pregnant for the third time, at the age of 43.

Mr. and Mrs. Cirillo were friends of the Savocas; in fact, they were tight as ticks, the four of them. They all knew each other through Tom's work. The Cirillos, who were older and wealthier than the Savocas, owned a factory in the Bronx. When Mrs. Cirillo heard about Jean's pregnancy, she was thrilled, so Jean asked her to be the godmother. Mrs. Cirillo presented Jean with a white wooden chifforobe for the new baby who was to be born in May of 1947. It was a gift of high quality.

On the left side of the chifforobe were four drawers top to bottom. On the right side was a miniature closet covered by a door. Inside the opened door on the top of the closet was a mechanism. It pulled straight out to become a rack on which a mother could hang her baby's clothes on miniature hangers. The mechanism retracted back into the closet space and the door closed neatly.

Jean and Tom named their baby Gloria. The chifforobe held her clothes, lotions, brushes and towels. When Gloria grew bigger, her things got too bulky for the drawers and closet in the chifforobe, so Jean and Tom got her more appropriate furniture. As for the chifforobe – well, it was a simple, lovely piece, given to them by dear friends, so Jean and Tom decided to hang on to it. They stashed it in the basement of their Queens house.

Nearly ten years had passed since baby Gloria had used the chifforobe. By then, Gloria's much older sister Marian had met a man named Joe, a smart, affable teacher, and an immigrant who came from Newfoundland. Marian and Joe fell in love. They had an August wedding and a Bermuda honeymoon, after which, aglow, they returned to Queens. It was just for a few days; enough time to pack their things in their car to move. Joe's new teaching job in

Virginia was to begin in September. Marian and Joe were anxious to find an apartment near his work.

They found out that they were pregnant around Halloween and decided to share their news with Marian's family back in Queens in person. When Jean heard they were coming from Virginia for a visit, she suspected. She decided that she and Tom would give Marian and Joe the chifforobe. She painted Glo's old white chifforobe an attractive dusty green.

After the long drive to Queens, Marian and Joe parked in Jean and Tom's driveway, and hurried up the lower steps in the front and around the house. They burst through the side door. In less than a minute, Jean and Tom learned that they would be grandparents.

"Oh, how wonderful!" Jean wept. Tom smiled, "Aw, congratulations, the two of you!"

"We have something for you," Jean said as she wiped her eyes. She showed them the newly repainted chifforobe.

"It's gorgeous, Mother! So useful, too," Joe gasped gratefully, looking in the drawers and closet. "This was Glo's? It looks brand new. We'll put it to good use, won't we, Marian?"

"What a color! Of course, we will. Oh Mother, Daddy, thanks so much! It's perfect." Marian's fingertips glanced the top of the chifforobe.

"You remember it was white for Glo," Jean said, "but you should have a fresh start with it."

Marian and Joe drove it back to their Virginia home. Their baby arrived in June of 1958. She was named after Grammy Savoca, and the chifforobe saw her through her infancy. When the second baby, like the first, was a girl, Joe painted the chifforobe pink. Perhaps this influenced what happened over the next few years: Marian and Joe had two more baby girls, four in all. Over the years, Mrs. Cirillo's gift of the chifforobe to Jean and Tom held the clothes, booties, and blankets that two mothers, both Jean and her daughter Marian, had used for five baby girls – from Aunt Glo to her four nieces, Jeannie, Dar, Audie and Emmy – the last of whom was born in 1965.

The chifforobe was pink when Marian's oldest girl, Jeannie, was almost ten, and her youngest girl, Emmy, had just turned three. One dark February evening, in their Virginia home, the four girls' father, Joe, fell suddenly to the floor.

At the hospital, the doctor said Joe was gone. Within minutes, a nurse asked Marian who they could call for her. Like a soldier reciting a name, rank and serial number, she intoned, "Five-one-six-seven-three-two-three-eight-six-two." It was a Long Island number for her brother Tommy and his wife Ann. The nurse dialed the number, then handed Marian the phone.

When Tommy got on the phone, Marian said blankly, "Hi. You won't believe what's going on here, but Joe died."

Thinking there was some egregious mistake, Tommy said, "No, he didn't."

Marian said, "I know it sounds crazy, but Joe definitely died. I'm standing in the hospital with the doctor."

"Let me talk to him," Tommy said. Marian gave the phone to the doctor. The explanation Tommy needed took only a few moments. The doctor gave the phone back to Marian.

"I'll be there as soon as I can," Tommy told her.

Ann was only a few steps away from the phone, so she had heard Tommy's horrified responses to whatever it was that Marian was telling him. Tommy spoke quickly. Then he and Ann moved as one by instinct, reflex.

Minutes later, they dropped their two children off at their cousin's house. The cousin lived around the corner, with her husband and five kids of her own. She didn't hesitate to take Tommy's two.

Tommy and Ann sped from Long Island to Virginia on I-95. In the darkest part of morning, they arrived in Marian's driveway, then walked in. The four girls were sleeping or pretending to be asleep. As the adults fell into each other's embrace, they all fully grasped that it was real, that Joe had died, even though he hadn't yet reached his 46th birthday. Even though Marian and their four little girls needed him. Even though, with his solid commitment to all of them, his loving personality, and his sense of humor, he was the last person that anyone thought could die. Joe's untimely death would upend everything.

Virginia was as different as it could be from New York City. As newcomers, Marian and Joe had tamed it, and made it their home. But now, on the morning after Joe died, Marian said she wanted out. If they would be without Joe, then they would be without him back in New York. So, that day, Ann carefully packed the girls' necessities—their clothes, their dolls, their pop beads, their ponytail holders. The very next day, Tommy and Ann transported their four nieces and Marian, with all the things that the five of them needed most, including their car, from Virginia, back to Queens, back to the girls' grandparents, back to Jean and Tom. The girls' Aunt Glo had married then moved away, so Jean and Tom, gingerly, lovingly caught the five broken eggs and filled their own empty nest.

In the next few days, Marian decided that she and the girls would stay temporarily in Queens with their grandparents to let the three oldest girls finish out the school year at the same Catholic elementary school that Glo had attended. Coincidentally, right before the crisis with Joe, Jean and Tom had been envisioning Tom's retirement in the next year or two. They were looking forward to a change from the city, envisioning a country life out on Long Island. So, they all pulled together: the grandparents, Jean and Tom; their daughter, Marian, with the empty space beside her where Joe was supposed to be; and their son and his wife, Tommy and Ann.

They all agreed that when the school year ended in Queens, Marian and the girls would move out to Long Island for good. Luckily, Tommy was a contractor who was talented, industrious, a perfectionist in his work, and a caretaker where family was concerned. They planned that Marian and the girls would move into a new house that Tommy would begin building immediately—a new house next door to his own, where he lived with Ann and the girls' two cousins.

Since Marian's three oldest were used to Catholic school in Virginia, she would take the summer to find a Catholic school near their new Long Island house, with the idea that the girls would begin school there in the fall. For the coming school year, Marian would stay home with Emmy.

Then, when Tom would retire, Jean and Tom would sell their Queens home so that they could move out to Long Island, too. Tommy would build his parents a new house right next door to the house he was building for Marian. It would be three in a row: Tommy on the corner, then Marian in the middle, then Jean and Tom on the next corner. They all knew that nothing they could do would make up for Joe's absence, but everyone's instinct was to bring the family together, into close proximity. This arrangement, they reasoned, would, at the very least, create support for Marian, who would have ready help with the girls anytime she needed it. The plan for Marian and the girls to settle permanently on Long Island was set.

In the weeks to come, back in Virginia, in the house where Joe had died, the movers packed whatever was left, lock, stock, and barrel. The pots and pans, the silverware and dishes, the sheets, the towels, the summer clothes, the small organ that Marian and Joe had played, the table upon which it had sat, the living room couch and chairs, the master bedroom set, the girls' beds and dressers, Emmy's chifforobe. It took a few months, but one July day, it all arrived at the new house on Long Island. The new house inhaled all the Virginia things into the rooms, the closets, the cupboards.

Emmy used the chifforobe as each of her sisters had. When she grew stronger and taller, like her sisters, she became impatient with the silly thing, with its drawers that fit only baby items. The mechanism now shrieked in protest when it was pulled out; worse, it made only a weak little rack that could hold only doll clothes. The chifforobe was useless, so it became a plaything.

The girls removed its drawers as if they were toys. They sat in them, carried the smallest girls in them, even turned them upside down then stood on them so they would be taller. The girls loved the closet covered by the tidy door. They hid whoever would fit inside. They had them burst out on cue, surprising adults, making them catch their breath. When, finally, the girls had broken a drawer, written on the chifforobe's closet door with red crayon as though it was a piece of poster board, then cracked the closet door off its hinges, the girls pushed the chifforobe into the garage of the Long Island house.

The garage was the very last place where a thing could be before it would be kicked to the curb then ultimately gone for good. The garage was a wasteland of spider webs, cricket carcasses and moisture. Exiled, the chifforobe sat there from the early 1970s till 2011. Parts of it got warped then buckled.

But...no one threw it out.

2

Whisper Sweet Nothings

Leslie Ellen Archer

"Oh, she has a beautiful mane." Our vet lifted Whisper's head from my lap to slide off her halter. Her big brown eyes looked at me through those flaxen bangs. She lay in the corner and she nickered so softly no one could hear but me. At her neck, the vet plunged the needle in, emptied a huge vial of blue liquid pentobarbital into her vein. "The second dose."

Dr. Dart sat up and put her stethoscope to the flank of my thirty-year-old filly. A distant mournful howl from Halley, our red husky puppy, filtered down from the yard at the exact moment the vet pronounced. "Her heart has stopped."

Her big, willing heart.

For the past hour, I'd crouched on the soft bedding in the stall, leaning on the worn saddle her trainer, Ellen, had lent me. I rested my cheek against Whisper's soft ears and reminisced with her.

Remember the trail that follows the power lines? On the other side of LaFayette Road, we break into a gallop. Just before we reach the top of that long hill we have to decide quickly which way to turn. Left across the corner of the field into the woods trail that leads all the way to the ridge behind town. Or right, following those power lines up over the crest down through a deep gully that is sometimes a running stream, leading to the old cemetery. You choose, knowing my intent before I do.

Remember those running streams? The one we skirted all the way into the woods until we found a bridge of dry grass sufficient to cross? The time we turned back toward home just before the stable, crossed the road again, and spent an hour arguing about whether to cross a tiny rivulet snaking across our path? You won. Even when I dismounted and coaxed, stomped and yelled, you weren't going to get your feet wet that day.

There's a wider stream at the bottom of the ravine running all the way to the edge of town. A wooden bridge crosses it, water visible through slatted crosspieces. Way too scary. At the crossing, we argued some more, took a long drink together, and then triumphantly splashed across to pick up the trail on the other side.

That day, we followed the stream south, crossed Route 20 and kept on going, came upon a carnival of kids at the new firehouse. We stopped for some carrots, a lot of nuzzling, and oohs and aahs. Then we wheeled around, like the horses in the movies, and galloped off to the tree line, found a trail, and kept on going until it began to rain. Only then did we turn back and retrace all our steps, drenched, like the cowboys in the movies.

Remember riding the other way, up to the ridge that plunges to the next valley, all the way to the pond four miles away? Or sauntering to the end of our little road, crossing the field and taking old "refrigerator" trail to the lookout, skirting that huge field, and then switchbacking downhill through the woods to the railroad track. From your pasture at the top of the hill, we can hear that train rattling on the tracks every day: 11 a.m., 3 p.m., 11 p.m., and 3 a.m. Making the time.

Remember riding into such thick brush we had to back out?

Remember riding off every Wednesday morning to the stable for our lessons? My lessons, seated on Ellen's well-worn hand-me-down saddle.

"Ride her like an equestrian queen, she'll know what you want her to do," Ellen told me. She would shake her head when Whisper shied at the mirror or jumped at the tractor parked outside the open barn door.

"She lives with a donkey. What do you expect?"

Then we'd ride out that door, fly up the hill to the ridge, and see if we could run the whole way until we chose one of the many trails through the woods that led to field edges, up and down to the top behind the new windmill, across the road and onto the familiar trail leading home.

"Whisper," I breathed against her soft mane, "Remember?"

The morning light wandered across the wall of fluttering old show ribbons. Everyone thought they were Whisper's—she was so beautiful—but no, they had been won years ago by her old companion donkey, Ernie.

You loved that donkey, Ernie. You raced around the paddock frantically whenever we loaded him into the trailer to take him out for one of his events. Sometimes we ponied him with us on our trail rides. Up and down the hills, into the woods, he would follow us. The two of you broke out and took a few jaunts on your own, led me all over those hills on foot before allowing me to grab one or the other, hop on, and head home.

Marking the time. Whisper was well into her twenties, Ernie at least thirty-eight years old. On a cold February night that donkey mustered up the strength to lift the gate off his stall, break out and collapse in front of her stall. I sat with him until the vet came and gently eased the life from him. Whisper and I walked out, away from his frozen body, across the fields. Blades of frozen grass crunched under her delicate hooves. She was alone for the first time in her life.

When Whisper was six months old, a foal who had been trailered by her mother's side to a small horse farm south of town, I brought her home. I walked her away from the roads, over the trails, four miles to our little hillside place. Ernie the donkey was waiting, in a new barn we had built with salvaged old barn parts. For the next two years, we watched her glide around the pasture while Ernie furiously pumped his little legs to keep up. I walked her at halter, then sat on her back. I took her to the stable for "finishing school." They taught her proper gaits.

"She could show," Ellen told me. "Just teach her to set her head."

Maybe she could show, but not me.

Horses are herd animals. Whisper was lost without her donkey. I looked around and found a big, pushy pony named Mirage, to keep her company. The two of them got along just fine.

In the last two years, Whisper's fine legs had weakened. She stood daintily in the field with one of them cocked up, like a four-legged flamingo. On our last ride, she stumbled plenty. On the day after Christmas, she went down as I lifted one front hoof to clean it. It took five of us a full day of hoisting and pulling to coax her back up. In the end, she really got up on her own. Every time she fell after that, she really got up on her own.

Then she went down in the paddock. She dragged her back end fifty feet through the mud. Got herself back up. The next Saturday morning, she was down again in her stall. I went over to the stable.

"Call my nephew Mark," Ellen said. "If anyone can get a horse back on her feet he can."

Mark came three times in all; we heaved our weight at her rear end, hoisted her with a girth strap, coaxed her from the front.

"She's exhausted," he admitted.

Still trying with all her mighty heart.

So, I called the vet. She told me Whisper shouldn't lay there all night. Her body would start to shut down, it would be hard to get euthanizing medication into her bloodstream. The vet could be here in 45 minutes.

"OK, come."

In between frantic discussions of how we would deal with her 1200-pound body after she was gone, I had myself several good cries. Then I headed down to the barn, walking through the clean crisp air and in the barn door.

There stood Whisper at the gate.

"Leave her out."

The vet would turn around and head home that night.

"Mirage will keep her company."

There was a huge full moon. Whisper basked in it, out in the pasture with her companion pony, Mirage, by her side. All the next glorious day they walked and ate hay and niggled tiny shoots of spring grass. We were ecstatic, but we plotted her inevitable burial day. By evening the weather had turned as nasty as it could be, a biting wind, rain, and sleet. I put them into their stalls with hay and grain and fresh savings, not too much for Whisper who loved to roll.

Snow covered the hillside the next morning. Craig and I walked down to the little barn with trepidation and yes, there she was, again down in her stall, rocking and fighting to get herself up. Over and over, she struggled to raise her body with those weakened rear legs. By noon we knew. She was all done.

I stand in the stall looking out across the paddock. On the other side of the fence, we've planted a Norway Maple tree over Whisper's grave. If you are wondering how we got her 1200-pound body over there, that's another story. For now, I just want to reminisce with her again.

How'd you do it, Whisper girl? How did our time fly, up the hill and over the ridge? I couldn't hold on to it, in the midst of my own life. Even as we aged, even when you would limp over the slight bump leading out of your stall and trip out the door. Every time we reached the bottom of that hill, you gathered yourself up, and you ran.

Whisper, my beautiful red filly, you taught me to love simple pleasures. The sprint up the hill, your chest heaving as we near the top, your head toss and blow of pure joy as we slow to a prance. The wide-open gate to the big lower pasture, beckoning. The long draught of clear water in the morning as the moon sets, the sun rises, and the day begins.

Whisper and Ernie, 1991

Whisper

3

THE AMERICAN DREAM AND THE MORMONS

GEORGE BARBER

I first became aware of Hollywood in 1955. It was New Year's Eve, the biggest celebration of the year for the Scots and another opportunity to get drunk again. We were taken to the Cinerama Moviehouse and our tickets were paid for by Dad. As usual, Frank, my older brother, was in charge. He would turn seven the following week.

Once we were safely delivered inside the cinema, Dad crossed the street to The Globe, a pub where he and Mum were well known. We knew by the end of the movie they would be drunk and we would have to endure the painful journey home on the Number19 bus. Mum would be loud, singing, and cursing. Dad would be telling her to shut up, and the fellow passengers would be shaking their heads, and whispering comments about "what a disgrace" and "how shameful to neglect three young children." I would look out the window and pretend we were not with them, fleeing off the bus when we reached our stop, but at that moment, I had an escape from reality.

We were deposited into the care of a Hollywood musical Carousel for almost three hours. It was magical. Although I didn't really understand the plot, I was soon lost in a world of fantasy, color, song, and dance.

Like many millions of people, I was drawn into the illusion of the American dream through the eyes of Hollywood and ate it up hook, line, and sinker. I believed that everybody lived in a house with a garden and a picket fence. Doris Day and Rock Hudson were my idols. They seemed real, warm, and wholesome.

In American movies, when kids came home from school, Mom would always be in a great mood, wearing a crisp clean apron that never got soiled, happy to see them; there would be a plate of cookies on the kitchen table and a glass of cold milk. Mom would say "How did school go today Honey?" and if they had a rough day, she would always have encouraging advice and understanding.

After school, often we would come home and my mum would be on the couch with one of her nylons tied tightly around her head to ease the pressure of her headache. We knew to be quiet and not disturb her. My parents were scary and unpredictable and were quick with their hands. We were walking on eggshells.

We lived in a one-bedroomed, cold-water flat. The bedroom had two double beds: Mum and Dad in one, me and Frank in the other, and a fold-up cot for my sister Cathy. It had a wardrobe, dresser, and fireplace. There wasn't much room for anything else. Eventually, in the late Fifties, we got a TV, and during the long dark cold winter months, Dad would turn the TV in the living room around to face into the bedroom and we would all get into bed early and watch it together from our beds.

The fire was going and it felt warm and safe. All of us altogether. After they turned off the TV and fell asleep, I would often lie there staring into the glowing embers of the fire trying to hold onto that feeling of security and thinking about escaping.

We would wake up in a freezing room. We had our breakfast in bed as there was very little room in the flat. We took turns washing at the sink, which lived above the coal bunker next to the window. I think there were a couple of toothbrushes in a cup and the occasional tube of toothpaste.

My parents had established a pattern of drinking that would continue for the rest of their lives. They were hard workers. My mother was considered a great beauty in her time with long dark hair, and flashing green eyes often compared to the movie star Ava Gardner. She was gifted with a fine singing voice and after a few drinks could be easily coaxed to belt out a few numbers in the local pub. She was a weaver in a jute factory, part of the huge industrial machine that was the backbone of the UK working classes.

My Dad was a quiet drunk. He was a Rag and Bone man who bought scrap from the local farmers and resold it to the local scrap merchants. He bargained for old clothes from the gentry. He was very critical of me. I couldn't play football properly. I was unable to tie my shoelaces correctly, stuttered, sucked my thumb, and wet the bed until I was almost ten. Most Friday nights, after school, and Saturday mornings, Frank or I could be found holding a place for my dad in the queue at locally advertised Jumble sales held in Church halls. We would have to stand behind him as he made a run for the best bargains, then throw the garments over his shoulder for us to catch. We would get home late around 7 p.m. starving. My mother would repair the clothes, clean and press them, and take them to a local second-hand market where she rented a stall for the weekend to resell them.

They worked hard and drank hard. Their drinking went in cycles that usually started on Sunday afternoons when they decided to go to the workmen's club to play Bingo. After a four-day binge of constant drinking round the clock, by Wednesday they had drunk themselves sick. During this time we were on our own. We didn't go to school. I became the caretaker for the family, and we constantly squabbled with each other, squandering any money that was to be had on sweets and eating from the fish and chip shop while waiting for them to come off the booze.

Over the years, the cycle of drinking continued and the binges increased in length until they went the full week. We were so fed up with the broken promises they would make, after swearing off drink forever again. It always ended the same and life really felt hopeless. We had lost any trust in them we had.

Then, in 1960, we met the Mormons. We went to visit my Auntie Margaret and Uncle Jimmy one Sunday afternoon. They lived close by, about a ten-minute walk. They had seven kids and were our closest relatives. There was a lot of chatter about a group of people from a church in America called The Church of Jesus Christ of Latter-Day Saints; they were called Mormons. My ears pricked up immediately. "They are from AMERICA!" I wanted to know everything about them. My cousins said they would take us to the next service. Mormon missionaries had been visiting the neighborhood and spreading the word of Joseph Smith, their visionary leader who experienced a vision of God that had appeared before him in a forest in upstate New York, which led him to create and build the First Mormon Church in America.

I fell in love with them. They were late teenagers doing their two-year missionary service for the Church, but being a nine-year-old they appeared adult to me. They always had sweets to give and would say things like "you guys are so cute," and "we love the way you speak," but the biggest draw was no one smoked or drank in their faith. They were so clean and bright they even smelt differently! I would take deep breaths of air when around them and try to hold onto that feeling of goodness.

All three of us kids attended their meetings several times a week. They had a host of parlor games based on biblical stories and themes that I loved. The meetings were probably a couple of hours and seemed to always go so quickly, and I would think, "Why do the good times seem short and the bad times last longer?" They were American Gods. I decided people from America were different; that they made me feel hopeful about life. I'm going there one day!

A classmate of mine, Gordon Pullar, had been given an extended two weeks added onto the annual seven-week summer holidays to visit relatives in New York. It was all very exotic and I remember being very envious of him, that he traveled by boat to get to America. Air travel was not for the working classes then. He eventually sent a postcard to the class of a huge multi-story building that we were all in awe of. It turned out to be the City Hall building in Buffalo, upstate New York, not the New York City from the movies that I had fantasized and daydreamed about. But it was still America.

My sister Cathy and I continued to follow the Mormons devotedly. My cousins dropped out of the Mormon scene after my Auntie Margaret began smoking again. She'd gained a lot of weight, unable to control her appetite, and said the Mormons were a waste of time. We, however, went one step further and convinced our parents to let us get baptized into the church. My father went with us. It was a 20-mile drive from Dundee to Perth. We had been asked to bring a white shirt and trousers for the event, and a white petticoat for Cathy. We went to the local swimming baths in Perth. My dad asked us again if we really wanted to do this. We both said yes. I was nine or ten, Cathy close to eight. Frank didn't partake.

Looking back over the years, I would think to myself that my parents must have been a little crazy to agree to this. We were just kids. I had bought the whole illusion of the American way of life. I just had to figure out how to get there and escape this horrible, crazy life here in Scotland.

A few weeks later, after being baptized, one afternoon there was a knock on the door. It was a couple of the Mormon elders and they wanted to discuss the issue of tithing. My dad didn't know the meaning of the word. When they explained that part of the financial support for the Church was an expected ten percent or more of the congregation's salaries, he lit up a cigarette and, very agitated, said that there was no way he would be giving any hard-earned money to the Church. He told them in a few choice words to piss off. They left immediately, never to be seen again, and took with them part of my dream. I was devastated and heartbroken. I loved their goodness so much.

Almost twenty years later, I moved to Los Angeles and stayed with friends until I found my own place. A few blocks away from the apartment a magnificent Mormon Tabernacle was rising up into the sky, decorated with splendid spires, life-sized statues, and manicured pastoral grounds. One day I stood outside by the grounds there admiring the building and reminiscing about how the Mormons had influenced my life. Suddenly, two young missionaries approached me on the sidewalk. They said "Hello" and asked me if I knew about The Church of Jesus Christ of Latter Day Saints. I replied, "Yes," that I was baptized in Scotland many years ago but was not interested. They asked me why. I quickly replied with three reasons. I smoked, and drank, and I was gay: and knew that the Church excommunicated gay men. Stunned by my response, they simply replied, "Have a nice day."

It was a beautiful sunny day in Southern California. I still had to look for an apartment, get a job, and a car. No time to waste! I had to get on with my American Dream.

4

WINTERSTORM

HOLLY BESAW

"*Set your minds on things above, not on earthly things.*" *Colossians 3:2.* [1]

In February 2008, snow was falling and falling like I had never seen before and you could only see white beautiful snow, not even the road. The plow driver came trying his best to plow the driveway; however, he had to stop because the snow was so deep it ruined the transmission in his pickup truck. There were 8 plus feet/106 plus inches of snow!

I heard a scary loud noise at 3 a.m. during the storm. I walked throughout the house searching for the source. When I got to the kitchen, I saw the kitchen wall caving in. My husband and I rushed outside to see the roof of the house was collapsed. We put the cats and dog into part of the house that was not under the collapsed roof. They were confused and trying to get out.

---

1. All scriptures in this chapter are taken from the HOLY BIBLE NEW INTERNA-TIONAL VERSION Copyright 1973,1978,1984 by International Bible Society. Used by permission of Zondervan Publishing House. All rights reserved.

We brushed off the feet of snow on our SUV, going as far as we could, shoveling the snow that had fallen in just hours, snow coming over the hood until at last we saw the road. Driving on the side road ever so slowly to the main highway, we found one light in the dark snowy night an open, plowed gas station!

We called the insurance company and were informed that we had coverage for a natural disaster and asking us to call the fire department. We called the fire department and went back to the road by our home without even being able to follow our tracks as they were snowed over. The volunteer fire chief met us at our house where he examined the damage and told us it was not safe to stay. Here we were in the middle of the night with no family in the area, no motel in the small rural town, and no place to go. The fire department was generous in allowing us to stay in the firehouse until more of the town was open.

The day would truly show "The Lord will hear when I call on to him," Psalm 4:3. I lifted the situation up to God in prayer. We went to a local diner when it opened for breakfast, then to the SUV to make calls to work to use a personal day. One of the owners of the veterinary practice told us the pets could temporarily stay there. I had grabbed our tax information on the way out of the house and called the tax preparer; he had a morning appointment, another answered prayer.

The insurance agent and adjuster (bringing snowshoes) met us for lunch at the same local diner (the only dinner in the small town). They explained our insurance policy, including additional living expenses for us and our pets as well as giving us a check. The insurance agent and insurance adjuster went over to the house with us. We took the pet carriers we had and since we did not have enough carriers, we made a few trips to the veterinarian's office ever so slowly through the snow-covered driveway and recently plowed roads. The pets were scared and confused by the change in their routine with some of them crying in the carriers. The veterinarian's office set up a special area in the back (similar to making room for baby Jesus) with comforters, boxes, food, and water so the cats could be together. We were blessed with a motel to go to with the additional living insurance coverage, the clothes on our back, a computer, and a Bible.

For the days to come I lived by John 16:33: "In this world you will have trouble. But take heart! I have overcome the world."

The hotel was in the next county and about 45 minutes in good weather to our house. We were driving out of the storm. The first night felt a relief to be safe, in a warm bed, shower with toiletries, and a breakfast the next morning. We were able to go to a department store for clothing. The next day Sunday was my first outing by myself to church where they prayed. Later in the week, they offered us a gas card. My co-workers were generous in helping us recover.

On Monday morning, I returned to my students, which I enjoyed. I taught Early Intervention (students from birth to five with developmental delays) in their homes with a few students in a classroom. I was able to use the computer connected to a printer in the lobby to create and print teaching materials. On day six, the insurance company asked for the assessed value of the house and explained the house was a "total loss," meaning we were not going to be able to go back to live in our house again; our reality: we were "homeless." We said lots of prayers and asked many questions like, What do we do now? What do we do in the future? How do we navigate the next steps of our life?

Feeling blessed to have insurance, we had a check to pay off the mortgage and a check for the difference in the assessed value to take to the bank within days of getting the payoff approved. At the bank, we met with the manager. It took over an hour to complete all the paperwork and process paying off the mortgage. The house was now paid off and the property was ours. We prayed for the future and where God will guide us.

We discovered most of the restaurants in the area for dinner daily and weekend meals, saving the receipts for the insurance company. I was able to visit the pets a few times a week and called every day to check on them. It was a blessing to see them and give them all my attention, and hard to leave as they wanted to come indicated by them following me to the door of their area. The veterinary staff took phenomenal care of them.

God led me to donate the house to the volunteer fire department for training and a controlled burn so that they could use the knowledge in God's Kingdom. Using part of the house that was not collapsed, the department, along with another department from a neighboring town, performed two trainings at night, which we observed. It was the first fire for one of the firefighters. Later he became an officer of the department. At the beginning of the final burn, the firefighting priest said a prayer then the fire department burned the house to the ground. A neighbor sat with us as we watched our earthly house and memories burn while lots of firefighters were doing their jobs. The volunteer fire department checked on the property during the weekend.

After a few weeks at the motel, we found an apartment in the area to rent that took pets while we worked on rebuilding a homestead. The insurance company rented us furnishings with the additional living coverage. After praying without ceasing, we decided to sell the property and build a new homestead elsewhere. I continued to teach daily as we searched for a new property.

"For nothing is impossible with God," Luke 1:37.

We bought a 7-acre wooded lot in the area in October 2008, with the help of an overly patient realtor and a lot of prayer. We built over the winter with four subcontractors (heating/AC, plumbing, water, and alarm system). That snowy winter, while building, we ended up needing to use a payloader to move the snow for deliveries and to work on the house. The building permit was attached to a tree by the road in its own custom-made plexiglass box. We took trees from the property and had boards made at a sawmill. We worked five to six days a week with evenings at the local building supply company choosing materials to customize the house. It was exciting to see the progress! The house had a metal roof with a pitch so the snow would always fall off on its own.

By spring the ground was no longer frozen so we could bury the electrical and cable/internet lines to the house from the road, drill the well, and install the septic system to be able to move in during the spring of 2009. Evenings and weekends continued to be picking fixtures, cabinets, granite countertops, hardwoods from a local factory, custom tile inlay, appliances, paint, and furnishings.

God was present as the new dwelling was created. Over the years, God has blessed us with many cats and dogs. Each room has an angel and nativity in it all year round. The house has a prayer room with a prayer box, Bibles, journals (gratitude/sermon/prayer/Bible verses reflections), a scripture bulletin board, first grandchild's glider rocker, and a Christmas tree.

Douglas was one of the few items that was saved after the roof collapse and one of the first items brought into the new house. Douglas is a two-foot green fir tree that has two eyes and a mouth with a red hat. Douglas the talking tree is motion-activated to sing Christmas carols. Douglas is decorated with ornaments made by family members and students, in addition to special ornaments given to me by families I worked with. There is an angel with one student's name written on it, a handmade sleigh made out of popsicle sticks, a wreath made out of cereal, a heart made of dough, a train representing another student's favorite toy, a "best teacher" ornament, a teacher ornament that a student picked out for me, and two ornaments given as gifts from the real estate agent that helped with finding the property for our new home. All the ornaments hold a special place in my heart. Douglas the Talking Tree has a special place year-round in my prayer room next to the Nativity snow globe (white snowflakes fall in it like the snow in Upstate, NY).

"May the Lord bless you and keep you; may He smile on you and be gracious to you; may he look your way and give you peace." Numbers 6:24-26.

5

UNCLE PAT'S GARAGE

ANN SUTERA BOTASH

"Hello?" Mom answered groggily.

"Did I wake you up?" I asked, realizing I'd phoned before 7 a.m. and she was in bed.

"No, why? Are you disappointed?" She joked and cleared her throat.

"Sorry," I said.

Although over two hundred miles away, I knew she had been asleep and I felt an instant pang of guilt. She would never say she minded. I tightened my mittened hand around Casey's leash.

"I'm walking the dog."

"Is it snowing there?" Mom asked.

"Just the usual," I said. The snow had been blowing hard over the past several January days. "How's it there?"

"We've had a few inches," she said. Lately, Poughkeepsie, where Mom lived, was getting more snow than my region in Central New York.

My purple fleece headband held the phone earbuds snugly inside my ear canals. The lower half of my face was wrapped in a crocheted scarf, my own creation from leftover yarn. No one would buy such a thing. Stitches were randomly skipped, and rows were subtly uneven due to lazy counting. The mauve and blue colors, muted with age, were arranged in haphazard combinations.

When I was a teenager, my grandmother, Mom's mother, taught me to crochet. Grandma and Uncle Pat lived in the house on Stuart Drive. When Grandma died, Uncle Pat stayed until he was unable to live there without help. If she were still alive, Grandma would have expressed disapproval of the scarf. Tsk, tsk, she would say, as her eyes narrowly surveyed my work for errors. The memory of sitting on their living room couch, a pink crochet hook balanced in my right hand, came back with a flood of warmth. Grandma's lap was covered with perfect rows of a brown and ivory shell pattern, an afghan she ultimately gifted to me. A skinny length of twisted blue yarn dangled from my hook. Then, "Rip it!" Her voice echoed again from the past. Dutifully, I pulled a row and started again.

"I'm glad you called now. I need to get out early today too," Mom's words pulled me back from the glow of Grandma's living room. "I'm taking Uncle Pat to his eye doctor appointment."

Mom and her older brother, Uncle Pat, had macular degeneration and were losing their vision despite bi-monthly intraocular injections. Grandma suffered from this eye disease too, although you would never guess considering the abundance of blankets we were blessed with. Mom's vision was slightly better than Uncle Pat's and she could see well enough to drive him to appointments. On this wintry day, her vision would be put to the test. I winced at the thought of eye-shots and tugged the zipper of my boxy dog-haired jacket, pulling the collar closer to my chin.

The assisted living facility, The Landing, where Uncle Pat had been living for the past year, would have provided transportation to his doctor visits. He preferred my mother drive him. At 85 years of age, my uncle moved into the facility due to limitations caused by Parkinson's disease and his vision. It was too much to take care of himself, and the stairs of his raised ranch were an obstacle. At the ophthalmologist's office, Mom would let him off at the door, then she would hop out and help him shuffle into the building. She could park in the handicapped spot, but the walk to the door from the lot was too far for him. Instead, she left the car by the entrance, registered Uncle Pat at the reception desk, and settled him into the waiting area. She then moved the car to the lot and walked back to the waiting room. At 83, Mom's energy belied her age and sometimes led strangers to think she was Pat's daughter.

Mom often chatted with interesting people in the waiting room, usually holding tissues in their hands while their eyes dilated. She once met a 90-year-old who drove herself to her appointments, then received shots in both eyes, one right after the other, and drove herself home. The usual routine was to receive injections in only one eye per day. My mother reminded me about that woman and, forgetting I had heard it, launched into the story just as I reached the halfway point of my walk. We were both amazed at the fortitude needed to withstand needle injections in both eyes on the same day. Driving oneself home after such a trauma seemed like a bad idea. Dad drove my mother on her shot days. I hoped I inherited his eyes.

"So, is Uncle Pat looking forward to getting outside today?" I asked after she wound down the tale. Although not unwell, he'd been trapped in his room at The Landing for almost a month due to an influenza quarantine. A sign on my uncle's door when he first arrived said, "You have landed," with a play on words for the name of the facility. Unbeknownst to the facility staff, The Landing was also a play on words for Uncle Pat, who was a small plane pilot. Assisted living places were a little like purgatory, a landing spot before the next stop—a nursing home, or the "final" stop. Not that the facility was a terrible place to be, just kind of a limbo. Infectious disease quarantines created an even more challenging environment.

"I don't think so," my mother said, "He's a little confused. Did I tell you about last weekend? He woke me up just after midnight."

"You told me he called you one morning, and he thought it was night." I searched my memory and recalled my mother's concern about an unsettling phone call from Uncle Pat.

"Oh, that was another time. This last time, he called me and was upset he forgot his pills and missed breakfast. He thought it was afternoon, but it was after midnight."

My mother has trouble sleeping. Waking her up in the night would wreck her whole next day. Pat's new confused behavior seemed to be a sudden change. His physical decline probably began long before he was aware of his Parkinson's. Yet, mentally, Uncle Pat had always been as sharp as a tack.

"That's understandable since he's been stuck in his room for almost a month," I said weakly, not believing my own reassurance. "He could be depressed or just disoriented. Maybe the next time you bring him to his regular doctor you should mention this." I curled my fingers inside the palm of my mitten. It was a lot colder than I'd thought.

"Anyway, I still have to tell him I have an offer on his house."

"You haven't told him yet?" I stopped walking, as if Mom were next to me and I could turn to her to emphasize my surprise. Casey sat on the snow-covered road and looked up at me in anticipation.

When Uncle Pat moved out, Jim, who knew my parents from church, offered to purchase the house for a lower price than my mother and Uncle Pat were expecting. Uncle Pat's house was near the school, a nice neighborhood, and had easy access to main roads.

Jim waited a bit, and now that it was obvious Pat would not be returning home, he approached Mom again with an offer.

"No, I haven't told Uncle Pat. Not exactly, but I think he knows. In any case, Jim wants to buy it for his daughter and fix it up for her."

That sounded reasonable. Yet, the thought that Jim was planning to flip the house crept into my mind. The 1970s kitchen, with the lime green, yellow, and rust floral edging of wallpaper along the ceiling was crying out for flipping.

"Plus, we would not have to get a realtor involved, so we would save money there," Mom added, sensing my distrust.

"Does Uncle Pat know you are cleaning out his house?"

This was not easy on Mom. Since moving out last year, Uncle Pat often requested things he left in drawers, closets, cabinets, or shelves. When he left, he took his television, a few clothes, and his comfy chair, leaving behind the rest as if expecting to return shortly. Mom and Dad, with the help of my siblings who lived closer than I, already removed most of the furniture. We had all known Uncle Pat was declining physically. We had no idea the insides of his house mirrored his condition. When Uncle Pat gave Mom his keys, it was the first time in many years that she was granted access to his house. When he was younger, he used to joke: "If you are coming to visit, make sure to get your tetanus shot." The house was always spotless, and his words back then made no sense to me. Now, those words rang true. My family had been working on the house for weeks before I was able to get to Poughkeepsie to walk through.

"I ended up telling him because he asked me for some talcum powder from his bathroom. The bathroom was cleaned out months ago. He'd bought the extra-large containers of powder at Sam's Club, along with family-sized packs of several bottles of shampoo." My mother paused. They had made several trips to the local dump—truckloads—as well as donations to various local agencies.

"Did you buy some new talcum powder?"

I imagined my uncle, reclining in his chair at The Landing, watching re-runs of his favorite television show, *The Big Bang Theory*. All the while, on Stuart Drive, his house was being quietly emptied.

"No, I took some things back home to my house, like the talcum powder. I had a feeling he might ask for it. But I told him, 'Pat, you don't live there anymore, we have to get rid of everything if we are going to sell it.' He gets it. I don't think he thought he would *never* go back, though. In his mind, everything is exactly where he left it. He's the only one who knows where!"

Mom was shocked to see the disarray of his tools and partially finished projects in various rooms throughout the house. This was not the organized and meticulous Uncle Pat we knew.

While I was home over the Thanksgiving holiday that year, my mother brought me to Uncle Pat's house and began in the garage where many articles were being staged for sale. She lifted the one-car garage door over our heads and a musty smell nearly knocked me over. I wondered how Mom spent so much time there without succumbing to her allergies. Large pieces of equipment lined the walls. As my eyes adjusted to the darkness, a model wooden airplane suspended from the ceiling over one of his workbenches came into view. It was a perfect replica of a real plane. Above the tiny plane, the wing of an unfinished light aircraft spread above us, next to rows of darkened fluorescent fixtures. He had been building a "one-seater" experimental plane. He said two seats would never be needed, since who would fly with him in an experimental plane? I yanked on a fixture pull-chain swinging at eye level, only to remember the electricity was shut off.

I would later learn that the pieces of dust-covered equipment were expensive woodworking and welding machines. Anchored to workbenches, they stood ready to weld or scroll or cut. This was the workshop of an expert craftsman. Measurements were jotted on scraps of paper, instruction manuals were open on benches, and sharpened pencils and tools lay still, as though anticipating a job. Mom reminded me that these tools were bought pre-Internet and were not as available then. Researching the purchase of just the right tool involved a trip to the bookstore or library and a mail-order catalog.

An entire room was devoted to stained glass. Over the years, he created and gave away numerous exquisite table lamps. Mine had been a housewarming gift for my new home with my husband. The jewel tones and graceful daffodil designs continue to light our foyer.

My mother had stacked a pile of instruction manuals and other "How-To" books near the garage door, ready for a donation drop-off at the local library. I opened one, a relatively new book, called *Aircraft Electricity and Electronics*, and glimpsed my uncle's penciled notes in the margins; arrows, formulas, and lines, some erased and overwritten. Uncle Pat, like Grandma, understood the importance of practice and details.

"Take what you want," my mother said, spreading her arms widely as if embracing the contents of Uncle Pat's garage. With my hands in my pockets, I slinked through the house, past artifacts like a shy visitor at the Uncle Pat Museum. A few hours later, I left with two items. One was a vintage ceramic dish, about the size of my palm, for grated cheese. The yellow triangular cheese shape, with cheerful pink cheeks and a winking eye on one side, made me smile. Uncle Pat and I shared a love of grated parmesan and guarded the dish of cheese between us during Grandma's Sunday spaghetti dinners. Grandma's dining room table, where many years ago those dinners were served, was piled high with kitchenware, paperwork, books, other odds and ends, and Mr. Cheese.

The other item was an unframed oil painting on canvas. The still-life of flowers in a vase, with a royal blue background, was signed and dated 1969. On close inspection, the reflection of light on the vase was not quite right. Painting was one of Uncle Pat's early artistic hobbies and this was likely an early attempt. He clearly didn't consider it satisfactory; it remained unframed, stored upright between the washer and dryer amid some incomplete paintings.

"Mom, do you think you could call me when you get home from the eye doctor's later today?" I asked as I turned off the road and up my driveway. Casey lurched forward a little, yanking the lead, and pulling me along. It was time for her breakfast and almost time for me to change my clothes and drive to work.

"Sure!" She said, and added for my sake, "Don't worry, the weather is supposed to clear up and we'll be okay. Bye now."

Reaching the door, I adjusted my misshapen scarf, pushing the edge down to uncover my face and take in a breath of warmer air. I momentarily examined those knotted threads that kept my nose from getting frostbite. Someday, someone would come across this loved and worn tangle of yarn in the sleeve of my dog coat, in a closet of my house.

6

ORIGIN STORIES

HARRIET BROWN

Long ago a planet spun through the vacuum of space. It burned and cooled, swelled and shrunk and hardened. Methane, carbon dioxide, and hydrogen sulfide coalesced around it, oxygen from the water, and became an atmosphere and gravity. Somewhere on its boiling surface a single cell tumbled through the muck, its nucleus and cytoplasm contained by an invisible membrane, and then many such cells, propelling themselves with long whiplike tails too small to see. They clumped into groups, morphed over millennia into sponges and jellyfish, worms and fishes with symmetrical bodies and heads that held a simple brain and a bundle of nerves.

Those brains steered their corporeal bumper cars, banging and blundering forward, expanding into sophisticated nervous systems. Big brains meant better survival and an awareness of time: the ability to imagine the future, to understand mortality. These new creatures knew they would die one day. They felt the terror of that knowing and did not understand what to do with it. A curse, a blessing, or neither—they had no choice, they had to feel. The electricity in those big brains made them—let them?—feel so many things: fear and rage, pleasure and purpose, the despair and the thrill of being alive.

And the feelings were so changeable, so fluid. Like anger, which could erupt in the time it took for a single neuron to leap a synapse. And grief, which never went away, just subsided from a jagged pain into an ache. Worry, which canted them into an unknown future they couldn't control. These feelings could disrupt the heart's rhythm, bring blood to the skin, fog the mind like tear gas so there was room for nothing else. While pleasure, contentment, bliss—these were much rarer, harder to name, ephemeral.

And what was the point of all those feelings? People argued and hypothesized but in the end found no answer. They told each other stories instead, stories full of emotions that gave their lives a sense of purpose. Feelings were their raison d'etres and their modus operandi. Not everyone—there were those who didn't buy it, who thought all feelings were simple byproducts of random discharges in their big brains, accidents of electricity and biology rather than guiding principles.

No one could say which group was right, and over time they gave up trying. What was left was veneration for the act of storytelling itself. Stories defined their lives and their afterlives. When their physical bodies died, the stories others told about them continued to float through the world, growing paler and more translucent until they dissolved on the tongue of the air. It troubled people that they would never see or hear those ghostly versions of themselves, never know them or control them. They tried while they were alive to catch glimpses of those afterstories. They held ceremonies to imagine their future ghost selves.

They spent their lives trying, and failing, to know the unknowable. They invented rituals that might let them foresee their own endings. They analyzed the stories of the recently dead. But people's stories often took surprising turns, and there was no predicting those. They had to come to terms with the not knowing. A few took that to extremes, making a virtue of their mystification, their frustration. They sanctified it, built temples to it. They devised a symbol to represent it, which they inked onto their skin and carved into their gravestones.

But most people came to fetishize everything to do with stories and storytelling. There were schools of thought about story structure, pacing, tone, and diction, belief systems that people lined up to defend or attack. High Storytelling, for example, was considered sacred, an activity done after hours of chanting and meditation. High Storytellers used only polysyllabic words, creating winding strings of mellifluous sentences that rose and fell like breath passing through the body. They believed there was only one appropriate position for telling a story—sitting cross-legged on a pillow on the floor, palms held up and to the sides—and only stories told that way were considered true.

Low Storytelling could be done anywhere at any time in any position. Low Storytellers competed to make their listeners react, the louder the better. Audiences at Low Storytelling events farted and burped and shrieked with laughter, outdoing each other to create a barrage of sounds that left them drained and satisfied. Meanwhile, small groups of non-believers reminded one another darkly that there was nothing special about storytelling, that it was just one of the odd facts of their neurobiology, meaningless except for the momentary pleasure or pain it induced.

There were years when the High Storytellers dominated the planet, passing laws confirming their view of this holy element of life. Anyone telling a story without the proper rituals could be sent to prison. In other times and places the Low Storytellers came into power, and then anyone who (inadvertently or not) used any of the

High rituals when telling a story could be banished or even killed. Those in the middle tried to attract as little attention as possible, passing for High or Low when they could, going underground when they couldn't.

Toward the ends of their lives, most people let go of their allegiance to High or Low Storytelling. The real power of story was the way it connected them to their own feelings, even the painful ones like rage and sorrow. The artists were astonished to see their paintings and poetry and music transform, made clearer and more powerful in ways they didn't understand. The philosophers grew bored by the questions that had informed their work, turning instead to gardening or long walks. Businesspeople lost interest in making money, the ever-widening concentric circles of growth, and wondered why they'd ever found it so compelling.

Emotions broke the tidy boundaries of their bauplans, the bones and blood and meat they inhabited and that kept them separate from one another. Listening to a story, they forgot they were born alone, lived alone, and died alone. They didn't just understand that they were connected to every other creature in the world—they inhabited that connection. They were alive. They were alive now. That was really all that mattered.[1]

---

1. Some of the information here is synthesized and condensed from the wonderful book *The Deep History of Ourselves: The Four-Billion-Year Story of How We Got Conscious Brains* by Joseph LeDoux. Any errors are mine.

7

The Bionic Woman

Susan Burgess

The day after Labor Day always came too quickly when I was a teacher. Despite all the work preparing over the summer I never felt ready for the first day of school and yet I can see myself standing at the door of my classroom, #27, looking out over the playground with class about to begin. The year I recall fondly is 1977, which would be my fifth year of teaching elementary students. I was excited to be assigned a third-grade class and anxious since the year promised to be unusually demanding.

There is a phenomenon that can happen in any school, in any district, in any state. It happens when planets align and there is a random assembly of kids that, from the time they enter kindergarten together until the time they move on to middle school, they exhibit a collective personality and acquire a formidable reputation for disruption. This group makes teachers laugh harder, worry more, and have their patience tested constantly. It is not uncommon for one or two students in a classroom to cause concern, but it's rare when a group of kids can, as a whole, conduct themselves in such a way that teachers consider retirement at the very thought of having a classroom populated by "the group." And not just one classroom but the whole grade level.

The incoming class of third graders about to enter my classroom that year was a part of the group of kids exactly like that. They moved through the school like bulls charging through a canyon, eager to get through and out the other side. They were legends in the teachers' lounge and the stories of their antics and disruptive behavior were passed from year to year as they moved from one grade to the next leaving teachers exhausted and filing cabinets full of reports. Many years later I would change careers and find myself giving presentations to corporate executives, always causing some anxiety, but I never felt the kind of worry and uneasiness that I experienced on that day when I was about to greet my third-grade class of eight and nine-year-old's.

The previous week the faculty and staff had returned to set up classrooms, engage in faculty planning meetings, and generally prepare for the new academic year. We groaned at having to attend so many meetings but, looking back, I think we all secretly enjoyed the comradery and time with each other without the difficult responsibilities that would descend on us once the year got underway.

It was during one of these meetings that the second-grade faculty who had taught "the group" the previous year, presented the three third-grade teachers with a huge bottle of aspirin and a note saying "We loved them all and happy you have them now!"

"Strange, they are all great kids and smart," Marilyn, the principal, said, "but man-oh-man, put them together and it's like a powder keg ready for a match."

I had been recruited for a teaching position near Anaheim, California, in 1972. I moved from Michigan leaving family and friends and I remember feeling a bit adrift for a time but after four years I was even growing accustomed to the Southern California climate with temperatures in the high 70s, even 80s, in September. Even the school buildings were set up strangely. Due to the year-round moderate climate all the classrooms opened directly to the outside with no interior hallways, just sidewalks to connect the rooms.

As I watched the kids from my classroom door, in spite of my anxiety, it felt good to face the coming challenges with a few years of experience and a bit more confidence. The children were playing tag, chasing each other, giggling, and laughing. The primary playground, for first, second, and third grades, was a sea of disorganized exuberance. New shoes and sneakers, white tee shirts, jeans, khakis, and shorts in every shade, all still mostly clean, painted the field in a blur of activity against the brown treeless horizon. Baseball caps bobbed around adding vibrant color. Some of the girls wore skirts and dresses, first-day attire, and everyone sported a backpack ready for homework that may or may not get done.

Many of the kids about to enter my classroom knew me because I had been a first-grade teacher two years before. They were a collective handful. I recalled the incident with five first-grade boys when they somehow got stuck in the girls' bathroom and even the janitor had difficulty setting them free. They had tried a weird magic trick on the lock using rocks and sticks and broke it. It had been my first-grade classroom where the squirrel escaped from the cage, a show-and-tell project gone wrong. We all had to evacuate while animal control came to our rescue. No one ever found out how the cage was opened not to mention how the kids caught a squirrel in the first place.

It was also in that first-grade class while we were engaged in small group reading practice that one of the girls raised her voice, "Ms. Burgess, are you married? Ms. means you're not married, right?"

She sounded alarmed. This had obviously just occurred to her and she felt compelled to get to the bottom of what was troubling her.

The class stopped and waited for my response.

"No, Marta, I'm not married."

I was seated with a group and wanted to get back to the students. There was something in her voice, though, that told me this wasn't going to be easy.

"Well, who buys your stuff?" she asked. "Your dad, right?"

"No, my dad lives in Michigan. Remember I showed you on the map. I buy my things," I stood up.

"No, I mean like refrigerators and cars and hats and stuff."

The students were now engaged in the question of the day, "How could Ms. Burgess possibly live life without a man to help her?" They were all shouting out their own concerns about my ability to manage without a husband or a dad. It seemed reading groups were over for the day and, following their lead, we moved on to life lessons in finances, employment, and just a little bit of women's rights.

Some of these same kids from two years before were now in third grade and about to greet me as their third-grade teacher. They were hovering around the door as I thought about these scenes from the past. They had only been first-graders then, what would they be like now? According to their second-grade teachers, they were only picking up steam.

I was looking at some of the familiar faces when the bell rang and the children began to form lines in front of the doors. The notion of "lining up" was a challenge for them, having had a summer of freedom. I looked at the lines in front of the other classrooms along the sidewalk; first graders, lined up, second graders, lined up. Then there were the three third-grade lines. For these kids it was more like push, then shove, then try to stand still. Even when they worked at standing still they remained in constant motion.

This was the class that was attempting to line up outside my door. I knew from previous years and their reputation that they were smart, rambunctious, loud, and defied their teachers' abilities to have that all-important "classroom control." Individually they were each unique, intelligent, and clever but when you put them all in the same room they erupted into an energetic bundle of chaos.

I had worked on lesson plans for weeks and I had studied their records to make sure they received the appropriate level of instruction. My classroom was set up with carefully constructed bulletin boards, art supplies laid out on counters, science equipment organized on shelves, and the student desks arranged in pods. I felt ready for the students to venture inside.

I ushered them into the room, greeted each child, and even got a few hugs. I collected stragglers slowly heading to the door from the playground, two boys and a girl who felt it necessary to get in one last punch and kick before giving up on summer.

Once they were all accounted for we did a quick introduction and I got them started on a game I had devised, a treasure hunt to find their assigned desk. This became controlled chaos but got them engaged. I stood in front of the room watching the noisy, boisterous group mostly trying to follow the rules of the game. As I watched I noticed the arrangement of the room near the door and a very large cabinet that I could see was out of place.

As the kids were involved in the hunt, I considered the six-foot by five-foot shelving unit I had stationed at the entrance of the room. Though it appeared to be part of the room structure it was actually movable. Both sides of the cabinet could be used, one side for coats and the other side for books and supplies. I had placed it a few feet from the entrance so that the closet side faced the children as they entered and was easily accessible for jackets and hats. As the kids moved around the room, however, it became apparent that this placement closed off the classroom from much of the light the door provided. The children were busy and relatively occupied. I was focused on the misplaced cabinet.

It's important to note that this was in the 1970s and the era of Lee Majors and the "Six Million Dollar Man," an extremely popular television series that the kids all watched and often acted out when they were playing outside – inside too, to their teacher's dismay. The series was about a man whose life was saved using special cybernetic body parts and implants. He became superhuman, fighting criminals and saving the innocent. In addition, the "Bionic Woman," starring Lindsay Wagner, was a spinoff series. Her life was also saved with cybernetic reconstruction giving her super powers as well. This gave students of both genders opportunities for roleplaying their action heroes.

Twenty-five preoccupied children barely noticed as I walked to the back of the room to address the room's design flaw and the over-sized offending cabinet. With a great deal of force and strength, putting my legs into the effort, I moved it out of the way of the door to a new location, a few feet away. As I finished, I sensed the silence in the room, the kids had stopped moving or even talking. I turned to see every child sitting or standing completely still, all eyes on me. Realizing what I had just done what appeared to them to be an incredible show of force, I brushed my hands together and without saying a word I walked to the front of the room. We all carried on with our first day of school.

Later, as I walked to lunch, I heard from some of my colleagues that I had actually ripped a telephone book in half, something the Bionic Woman was known for. Clearly the children believed I had some super powers like their beloved bionic million-dollar heroes.

The kids never knew the large and, indeed, very heavy cabinet was on rollers tucked up under the casing that almost touched the floor. My colleagues and I had a new story about the notorious third-grade class and it was classic—teacher 1, kids 0—at least for the first day.

I remember I had very little trouble with my "classroom control" for the rest of the year. The boys were especially interested in helping no matter what the task. The students were attentive and generally eager to learn – most of the time. We studied the historic meeting of the Transcontinental Railroad linking the East and the West at Promontory Point Utah. We used it to do units of study involving math, science, reading, and art. Many of the parents got involved when we put together a three-foot by five-foot tabletop model of the actual site of the Golden Spike. We spent months studying all aspects of the event, what led up to it, how difficult it must have been, and who was involved. The children were so proud when we won first prize at the regional math and science fair. When they channeled their energy, they were a force and I had to work hard to stay ahead of them. Once or twice I saw several students try to move the cabinet when they thought I wasn't looking. I had locked down the wheels so that cabinet wasn't going anywhere.

There were a few incidents, like at Halloween with the fake blood and the time several boys got lost on a field trip for a heart-stopping twenty minutes. A group of girls, who could never stop talking, had discovered creative ways to annoy the boys. That was a distraction for months until the parents got involved. The children were physical with more than the usual hitting and name-calling that needed a strong referee but for the most part, we all got along and made it through the year with more smiles than tears. Their grades showed progress as well.

My display of strength was certainly not intentional but it had an effect that still makes me smile even so many years later. Now the aging process has settled in around me like a thick coat – warm and comforting with many pockets for memories. Like many of us over sixty, I have had knee replacement surgery. Too many miles as a runner? Too many downhill ski trips? Whatever the cause I am grateful that we have the doctors and the technology to replace parts that no longer work or cause us pain. According to OrthoInfo.com sponsored by the American Academy of Orthopedic Surgeons, there are approximately 790,000 knee replacements each year and a total of over 490,000 hip replacements. This doesn't include the progress made in shoulder, ankle, elbow, and wrist replacements.

While I am not the Bionic Woman with superpowers I am somewhat scientifically reengineered! And, I fondly recall when a wonderful, innocent, beautiful group of third graders thought I was strong enough to guide them anywhere.

8

MINDING THE GAP

KAREN C. CHAMIS

I sat comfortably behind my teen daughter and her best-friend-of-the-moment watching the New Jersey scenery speed by. The train accelerated as it left the congested tracks surrounding New York City. We had spent the day wandering the city in celebration of my daughter's 16th birthday and, based on the giggles from the seat in front of me, the trip was a success.

Lunch was at the Hard Rock Café, and then the girls saw the matinee of the musical *Spring Awakening*, just before its last curtain in 2009. While the girls watched a musical steeped in the complexity of coming-of-age in 19th-century Germany, I waited outside on a nearby bench where I could knit and practice the ancient hobby of people-watching. It felt good to be on my own for a bit. Both girls had done their best to ignore my presence throughout the day unless money was needed. I understood my role was purely utilitarian. I was only the financier and chauffeur for this grand birthday event.

Now we were heading home. Sitting behind them, watching the world fly by, I was caught up in the rhythm of the train and the sounds that accompanied it. At every stop, this wonderfully sonorous (if mechanical) female voice would announce the station, followed by the caution to "watch the gap."

I had been on other trains, in other cities. In England, the phrase used to warn passengers about the space between the train and the platform is to "mind the gap." I find this phrase requires a bit more introspection than its American counterpart to "watch the gap." To mind something isn't to simply see it, but to adjust accordingly. When we are instructed to "mind our manners" we are being told to see what we are doing to reflect on the appropriateness of our actions and to change them as necessary. Being told to "mind the gap" is to do the same: see, reflect, and adapt.

The laughter in the seat in front of me intensified, and I found myself reflecting on my role as a parent and the distance that was growing between myself and my daughter. I had worked with teens and young adults for most of my life leading youth educational programming in everything from zoos to retreat centers and understood the need for differentiation on her part. It was normal for her to want to spend more time with her peers, to not only separate from her parents but also to expand her own experiences as she began to figure out her identity apart from our identity as a family. I had taught parents about the developing adolescent brain and how opposition to parental authority was natural. I knew she was doing the work of growing up regardless of my readiness to allow her to do so. Our work as parents was to recognize this and to see, reflect, and adapt to the changing abilities of our children.

None of that prepared me for my own feelings about this ever-growing gap.

This evolving chasm between adolescents and parents isn't marked with yellow paint, bright signs, or a patient announcer reminding us of its existence and to take care. This gap, brought about by raging hormones and differing priorities, is brought to our attention in battles for control and autonomy. The ever-widening gap makes it easier to see... if not easier to mind.

My husband and I had raised our daughter to be a fiercely independent young woman in a diverse community, and we knew she was at a point in her life where she needed to wander a bit from her established home and sense of self. At this point in time, she was at a place where peer relationships, even those best-friends-of-the-moment, were critical.

I knew this. I also minded this.

Although we continued to work toward the moment when she would be capable of living on her own, our focus had always been on her development. Our hope as parents was that the foundation that had been laid over many years would be enough. For the first time, I realized that this growing gap, first emotional and then physical, would have an impact on me as well. I recognized my own need to focus inwardly, to "mind the gap" more intentionally.

The train pulled up to our station, and my daughter reacted to my tapping her on the shoulder with her patented eye-roll and a harshly whispered "I know, Mom." The girls got off the train after me and took their time walking toward the car. I remember sitting in the driver's seat as they slowly moved toward the car while I considered what my role would be once I was no longer needed. Someday soon she would be walking to her own car, and I wouldn't be in the story at all. Apparently, I had my own work to do if I were to find a way not to mind it.

***

Twelve years later I traveled to Atlanta, Georgia to see my daughter in a community theater production of *Spring Awakening*. She had recently relocated there with her fiancée and was balancing an evolving career in higher education with time with friends on stage.

Watching her perform brought to mind her birthday trip to New York. It wasn't lost on me that she had been the same age as the young person she now portrayed on stage. The show was brutal and beautiful in its exploration of the universal themes of teen sexuality and the cluelessness of the adults that surrounded them. Sitting there, applauding with the others in the audience, I affirmed that both of us had played these parts in our relationship. Together we created that necessary gap for her to become the incredible woman she is today.

There is still a gap between us, but we both do the work of minding it with visits, texts, and phone calls. The gap that I once perceived as an albeit-necessary threat now energizes our relationship as we continue to discover all the ways in which we are different, as well as the many ways we are the same. My role has changed. I'm no longer the woman with the credit card and car keys.

I'm just a mom—and I don't mind that a bit.

9

WORMS

Gwenlyn Davis

"You run differently with fear than you do with courage." Marisa Sutera Strange, Masters runner, champion.

On a snowy evening in 2010 when I was fifty-five, weary of the track I'd been on, I hauled myself to another new breast cancer support group hoping to learn something new. It was almost a year since my first diagnosis. I longed to experience my previous self, the person I knew the year before.

With the end of complicated treatments: surgery, chemo, and radiation, I was free from that unrelenting regime, yet I had not found liberation. Chronic, miserable discomforts lingered every day. Nerve damage changed the fabrics I could wear. Chemo brain gripped me in a haze. I questioned my doctors, "How long will this last?" . . . with no concrete answers.

During those nine months, I often whispered to myself, *focus on the positive,* and gave attention to each warmhearted, helpful gesture along the way. I'd gone from healthy to enduring debilitating remedies, and now at this latest juncture trying to recapture wellbeing, I thought, *I've never been here before either* . . . as I tried to navigate my way back to me.

At the first session of this breast cancer support group were twenty or more strangers seated around a massive horseshoe table. All women. There was ample space between each cushy, swivel chair for bulky coats, totes, and purses. I appreciated the soft creamy lighting, too, atypical of a large conference room. After so many months of being in a medical grinder, I wasn't accustomed to being out, and not in the evening, then I thought, *I could take a nap.* In front of each of us, a 3-ring binder containing page after page of the 6-week itinerary fully mapped out, along with a pen and blank paper. This was unlike informal support groups I'd attended where a handful of survivors converged to talk about whatever came up. In those conversations topics often skirted breast cancer, which I found frustrating, and they rarely centered on tools for getting beyond. I was eager to hear these women tell their stories and find information.

We were welcomed to attention by a lean, serious-faced woman. I recognized her as a nurse from my surgeon's office. The year prior during my pre-op appointment she had kindly handed me a squashy pillow, also in the shape of a horseshoe.

In the surgeon's office, she had said to me, "You'll need this for under your arm after surgery. They're made by volunteers." The fabric was a cheerful embossed two-tone pink. While I was appreciative of the gift, I wasn't clear why it was essential. *One more thing I don't need to add to my clutter.* As I was toying with handing it back with a thank you, she said, "Many patients find that applying this with gentle pressure to the surgical site can be very helpful at reducing discomfort." She was, it turned out, correct.

This nurse was our facilitator for the evening and directed us to introduce ourselves, ". . . and please share a bit about your specific diagnosis."

Each story was unique. We'd all experienced the frightening big C, but not one mentioned how scared they'd been, or perhaps still were. Fear was an emotional glint in the eyes. In halted breath. Was understood. Throughout, there was a painful yet tender kinship that permeated. There was an unspoken alliance. An accord. I felt comfortable.

After our introductions, the nurse continued, "Now go around and tell us something you're most proud of." I heard one attendee after another say, ". . . my children." Others, their marriage. Not being married or having children myself, to me it felt a touch like cheating. I thought, *sure you're proud of them, but what about you?* I had things to say, but nothing so remarkable as children, itself a miracle. *I'm proud of my boyfriend?* He had driven me to surgery and chemo. I settled on something about finishing college and making it through breast cancer.

Our facilitator dished out reams of information about the next hour . . . the weeks ahead. Too much. My muddled chemo brain was drifting. Then her tone shifted, "I want you to think of a time when you had to be brave before you were diagnosed. Write anything. You won't need to share it here. Now we'll take five maybe ten minutes."

I closed my eyes. One memory shot to the surface like a submerged cork. On that day, the welcome breath of spring overshadowed everything. The earth was soft, moist, and ripe for giving way to new sprouts. The air, flooded with the brightness of the sun, was still cool.

***

Kickball in the street and impulsive escapades were the norm in spring, summer, and fall. Sometimes winter. My mother's warble often followed me as I scooted out through the front door, "Just be sure you're home for dinner. Six o'clock."

We lived in a neighborhood bursting with maple and elm trees that reached into the sky. The canopy lined our street on both sides and towered over backyards where impromptu games—that usually involved running—would erupt among a shifting flock of kids. By the time I was old enough to play beyond our yard, my older brother and sister no longer did, and my two younger brothers weren't yet old enough. For several years I was the only girl in the mutable herd. It was the 1950s and '60s in the middle of New York state, and unlike today, children were often sent outdoors to adventure for hours without the watchful eye of adults.

When we moved into our drafty old house, I was almost four. I had no notion of course that childhood challenges could offer fertile learning ground for life ahead. Nor did I have much appreciation for my very youngest years as I grew older. Not until I was asked to look back, back to a time when I had to be brave. I came face-to-face with a few moments that stood up to meet me. Moments waiting, perhaps, for me to return. There I found a lesson I'd never seen before, a lesson that had served me well.

***

My mother had shooed me out of the house to play, "And re-member, you are not allowed beyond our yard. Have fun. I'll call you in when it's lunchtime." I wandered aimlessly around the perimeter of our house, then just stood there in my plaid pedal-pushers and blue jacket, the zipper pulled up snug, feeling all smiles inside. My new slip-on navy sneakers were topped with a wide white band of elastic and a decorative red ship's wheel across the bridge of each foot, and made me feel special. I loved those shoes.

Moisture beaded from the loamy soil near my feet as I stepped lightly, trying not to crush the patches of tender green, or get my shoes dirty. I moved into the narrow, shaded side between our house and the one next door, where no one ever went except to hop on the single swing or to dash through. It was peaceful.

Stopping, I leaned my belly against the fat, rusty pole of the swing fixed in the ground, arms dangling. Then going limp as a rag doll, I let my ear settle against the cold metal. A few kids were out of sight deep in the back of our yard and I could hear their chatter and lulls. In the pole the sound was different; a muffled tin-can rattle. I lifted my head up, down, up, down, immersed in my discovery.

Tommy came into view from around the corner of the house, stooping, moving slowly. I felt a warm shine at the sight of him. He was almost two years older than me. Our neighbor on the drive-way side, with his mom and three older brothers, our families were across-the-fence friendly, and cordial but not close. So, Tommy and I weren't really friends, more like buddies who happened upon each other outside. He brimmed with laughter, adventure, and noise. And he made me laugh too.

My focus went to him, amusing himself, digging, collecting worms. He meandered over, a wash of satisfaction on his face to show me his treasure splayed out in his cupped fingers, but I cringed. I welcomed his attention; not the creepy-crawlers. They were disgusting. Scary. I turned my back. Tommy, all legs, popped in front of me, so I turned again.

"Go on, hold 'em. I'll put 'em in your hands. They won't bite. Go on."

"No, I don't want to."

"Come on!"

"No-o-o-o, get 'em away. I don't like them."

His expression changed, like I'd seen on my older brother when he was about to do something awful like pounce on me, or tickle me until I couldn't breathe. Tommy pushed the squiggly mass closer.

"Stop it...Ssstop," I whined, but he kept it up.

He pulled back. He pushed them almost into my face. He withdrew them again. With his next push, I took a step back but was afraid of what he might do if I tried to run.

"Come on, take 'em. Here, take 'em," acting like he might dump them on my jacket.

"Ssstop!" I shrieked. And ran. The chase was on.

Tommy stayed just behind me, snickering, which prodded me faster. Hearing him slow down, catch up on my heels almost on top of me, then back off again, I didn't know what he would do if he caught me. I ran hard like the wind blew, it felt like for my life, as fast as my legs could carry me around the house. I would be running forever from Tommy and his nasty handful of worms. There was no sign of anyone to help. Inside I was screaming but outside was silent. I wanted to run in the house but couldn't. I had been told to play outside.

Somehow, I had to make him stop. From somewhere arose a decision to stop, turn, and face Tommy and his worms, my arms outstretched before me, pudgy little palms turned up. I stood firm in my special sneakers. Showed him I was not afraid. Squinting, I braved the mess dropping into my hands. They were wiggling wild from their long hot ride in Tommy's clenched fists. The ugly worms tickled and it was awful, but I didn't wince and held them steady. Our stand-off over, I dumped the hapless creatures back into his waiting fingers. I had survived triumphant.

Other than for a game of tag, Tommy never chased me again.

***

I lifted my eyes from my paper at the support group seated around the table. Some were still writing. Other faces gazed over the room. Our facilitator said, "Alright ladies. I'll give you another minute or two to wrap up. Remember you aren't going to share your story here with us. It was meant for you, so, if you're not done you can finish up at home."

For a bit, I remained in my bubble. After fifty-plus years, I had just watched that little girl I once was, felt her uneasiness creep in, sensed her panic, recognized her pluck, and felt the victory. How proud I was. I knew that resolve. She is a part of me still.

Where, I wondered, does a fearful tyke find the grit to turn and face the enemy, especially after starting by running away?

I've needed courage many times since that day. And when I've needed to be brave, I have reached in, perhaps to her, anchoring in to do whatever was required to get through the best that I could, to survive, and hope, pray, I'll be ok on the other side.

Then I wondered if our first brave thing isn't the bravest simply because we've never been there before. Maybe any new fear is the most daring. For me, that day was a fine small lesson in digging in and digging deep to face whatever is on the path ahead or chasing from behind.

10

HALLOWEEN TREAT

CAROL DECKER

It was a gloomy day—the day before Halloween, 1957. Rain spit pellets of snow at the windows. The lights were on at 8:30 in the morning. Ellen didn't feel well and called work to say she wouldn't be in. She was eight months pregnant with her second baby who was due about Thanksgiving.

Adam and Ellen had moved to Knaul Street with their two-year-old son, Aaron. It was a first-floor flat with two bedrooms, a kitchen, a living room, and their own bath, no more sharing one. Ellen's uncle and wife, Virgie, lived upstairs with their little girls, who were four and three years old. Virgie babysat for Aaron.

Ellen was twenty-one and worked at an insurance company. Adam was twenty-two and in law school at Syracuse University. Her office was about a mile away. Most mornings they got a ride with Larry, the drummer in the group that Adam played piano with on weekends. Larry picked them up at 8:15, dropped Ellen off at work, then the two guys went up to the university. She worked from 8:30 to 5:00 with an hour for lunch. Then she walked home: uphill through an old derelict cemetery, around a curve, and six blocks down the street to their apartment. There were rumors that the graves in the cemetery were from epidemics of cholera and smallpox and people shouldn't walk there.

Physically Ellen was in great shape. But she was exhausted. It wasn't just the pregnancy. It was hard to work all day, and then give Aaron some quality time when she got home. Plus, there was cleaning and washing and ironing to keep Adam in his blue, oxford-cloth, button-down shirts.

After classes, he went to the library to study and came home late. Sometimes he walked down the hill from the university to his parent's apartment in the housing project for supper and to practice the piano. Then he went back to the library. To get home, he took a city bus from the university to downtown, then transferred to another bus.

Mostly it was Aaron and Ellen.

On this sunless morning, Ellen sent Aaron upstairs so she could go back to bed. She lacked energy. In the back of her mind was Halloween. She wanted to get a costume ready for him so he could go trick-or-treating. It was his first time out on Halloween and she wanted him to wear something cute and safe when they walked in the neighborhood.

In the early afternoon when Ellen went to the bathroom there was fresh blood on the toilet paper when she wiped herself. She called her good friend, Kitty, a big-boned farm woman from North Dakota, and a former nurse. Her husband, Wendell, was a thin, wiry man, very serious, and always ready to help someone out. Ellen and Adam had shared a bathroom with them in their first apartment.

"Call your GYN," Kitty said.

Ellen called, and Dr. Belkin asked, "Are you having pain?"

She said "No."

He said, "Take it easy, if it gets worse or your pains start, call me."

Ellen loved her doctor. He had been her OB-GYN during her first pregnancy. He was a no-nonsense doctor, with a sense of humor. The few times she called him on the phone, he gave her practical advice and put her at ease.

Ellen just felt lousy. She called her mother.

"Mom, there's blood in my urine, andI don't feel good."

"Ok." her mom said, "I've got some time today, I'll come and pick you and Aaron up and you can come here for supper. Leave a note so Adam knows where you are. Bring some extra clothes for Aaron, just in case."

At her mother's Ellen wasn't very hungry. She was up and down on the couch, trying to get comfortable. It got dark very early. She put Aaron to bed, they sang his prayers, like they did every night; "Father we thank thee for the night, and for the morning's pleasant light . . ." After the prayer, Ellen pulled the blankets up around his shoulders and gave him a kiss.

"Good night, honey. Maybe we'll have a new baby soon," she said to him.

When Adam got home from the university, after reading the note, he called Ellen, then he called Wendell and arranged a ride to his in-laws house.

Ellen was so relieved to see Adam. They hugged, and she grabbed his hand and wouldn't let go. She wanted him with her. This was not like her first delivery and she was scared.

Nora, Ellen's mom, made coffee and they sat in the kitchen waiting, wondering. Ellen wandered from room to room, feeling uncomfortable and logy. It was about ten that night and there seemed to be more blood in the toilet when Ellen went, so she called Dr. Belkin again and he said, "Come on into the hospital and I'll have a look at you."

Wendell drove them there.

When the doctor finished examining her he said to the nurse, "She's not the type of woman to have labor pains that you can time. She'll probably have one big pain. When she does, call me. I'll be in the doctor's lounge."

He remembered her first delivery, and it impressed Ellen.

Ellen had that one big pain at about 1:30 a.m. The nurse told the doctor, he scrubbed and delivered their second son at 2:45 a.m. on Halloween. The baby only weighed five pounds and was twenty-one inches long. He was spindly looking, with spaghetti-like bones. His hair was dark, lots of it. He'd need a haircut when he got home. His eyes were blue, dark blue.

Ellen was groggy when they wheeled her to a room in the maternity ward. Once she got in bed, images in her mind tumbled between wanting to take Aaron out for trick-or-treating, and the Halloweens from when she was a girl with her friends who lived on Smokey Hollow Road. They were nine years old and it was the first time their parents let them make the mile-long walk to the village to trick-or-treat. They had soap and toilet paper with them and they were expecting to do some tricks if they didn't get treats.

At the first house with a porch light on they knocked and yelled, "Trick-or-treat!"

The woman who answered the door smiled at them and said, "Come right in. You do a trick, and then you get a treat . . . "

Ellen fell asleep smiling, thinking, A Halloween baby! Trick! Treat! A month early!

Dr. Belkin came in to see her when he made his rounds in the morning and said, "It's going to cost you a little bit of extra money on your hospital bill. I had to have everything set up for a cesarean delivery in case the baby didn't come out fast enough. You lost quite a bit of blood too. So I've ordered three pints of blood for you. You'll feel terrific when you get home."

Adam came to see Ellen on Halloween afternoon. He held her hand, and after they kissed, he said, "My mother has been diagnosed with ovarian cancer. They don't think she has long to live."

She squeezed Adam's hand tight, and said, "I'm sorry. Your mother is a nice, likable woman. Too bad our sons will never know her."

Because of this, they decided to circumcise the baby in the hospital. What a relief! Ellen remembered Aaron's Bris, the Jewish service for circumcision. It was done on the eighth day at home, and he screamed.

Because of the blood transfusions, Ellen stayed in the hospital for five days instead of four. Adam was there every day. On November 3rd, he walked in and said, "The Russians have just launched another satellite. This doesn't seem like a good time to bring another baby into the world. They even put a dog in their spaceship. I'm afraid they're way ahead of us in the space race. It's a really scary time to be born."

A nurse with a tray full of thermometers was walking into the room to take Ellen's temperature. When she heard what he said she dropped the whole tray. Glass and mercury went rolling all over the floor. "Damn," she said. "I'm sorry, it just shocked me that the Russians are getting ahead of us. I'll get a broom and sweep this up."

"That's OK," Ellen said. "Whenever my mother broke a thermometer she would let me play with the mercury. It's loads of fun to watch the way you can split the mercury, and then push it back together."

They named the baby Brian. She nursed him, and when they got home he cried to eat all the time. She loved holding him and feeling his long fingers on her breast when she fed him, but she worried that she didn't have enough milk. He was so skinny. And the crying. She felt terrible. Where was all this energy the doctor said she would have? She just wanted to nap and sit on the couch.

Then she passed a blood clot. It was a Saturday night at about 8:00 p.m. Adam was out playing piano with his group. Ellen called her doctor. The doctor's answering service said they'd let him know. A short while later he called her.

"This better be important," Dr. Belkin said, "I was playing bridge and had a great hand. What's going on?"

She said, "I passed a blood clot, and I'm worried I don't have enough milk for the baby, he seems to be hungry all the time."

"Aren't you glad the clot's out!" he said. "How big was the blood clot? As big as your head?"

"No, it was little, like a chicken's heart," she said. She felt better already, just saying it was little.

"OK. You may pass a lot of small clots. Don't worry about it. If you pass a big one, the size of a lemon or orange, or start to bleed heavily, call me. Anytime. Tomorrow have someone go to the drug store and get the supplies to make formula for the baby. For every other feeding, give him formula. It won't be the worst thing in the world if you can't nurse him. Have a good night."

She sat on the couch. It was just the two of them, the baby and her. She nursed him and he fell asleep. She did too.

11

Leaning in and Falling Down

Shannon L. Farrell

I walked out of my office heading to the departmental faculty meeting with a stack of papers in hand. As the new chair of an ambitious committee supporting student learning at our science-focused university in central New York, I was eager to share our newest initiatives with colleagues. Also in hand was a clipboard, pen, and hot tea in a shiny metal travel mug – a mug declaring "Mommy Fuel" boldly across the front.

Halfway down the hall, I hesitated. I doubled back, juggling keys out of my pocket, hurrying back into my office to swap the mug for my water bottle. Halfway back out the door, my craving for warm caffeine outweighed the fluttery anxiety I had about walking into the meeting with my mug. Alongside the inexhaustible list of faculty obligations, I had a 2-month-old and a 1½ yr. old and I needed the energy boost. I turned back toward my office to switch again.

I paused to consider my excessive indecision. I was *nervous* about bringing a "Mommy Fuel" mug into a faculty meeting, a gift for myself meant to be an encouraging reminder of the dual role I now held. It felt like a subversive act. Some research suggests that the small, personal talk in the minutes before meetings begin is crucial to workplace rapport and satisfaction. Thinking back to the dozens of meetings I'd attended as a highly engaged junior faculty member, I couldn't think of a single instance when a colleague even acknowledged having children, let alone shared family stories. In hindsight, this was one of many moments that should have signaled something was amiss. At the time, it was yet another anxious moment I tried to tuck away and ignore.

Eighteen months prior in mid-2016, I sat down with university Human Resources to responsibly prepare, professionally, for the birth of my first son.

"You can apply for medical sick leave and use the sick days you have accrued," the HR employee stated.

Puzzled, and thinking I must have failed to articulate my questions in the right way, I tried again to ask what my options were for maternity leave. At this supposed bastion of progressivism, "we do not have maternity leave" was the surprising reply. I had accrued six weeks of sick time. My approved leave time would bump up against the winter break, giving me a small window of time when my teaching duties, at least, would be modest. I raised concerns that I would not be "on leave" by any normal definition. In my two years on the tenure track thus far, it was clear that the treadmill of expectations was unrelenting. I had deadlines for grant proposals to write to generate funding for graduate students, student research projects to design and oversee, dissertations to review, and scientific papers to write and seek to publish, all the currency we tenure-track faculty sought to survive the academic gauntlet for another year. I was concerned about liquidating all my sick leave during six weeks in which I would be tacitly expected to work from afar, regardless of my physical state. I was given no alternate options and saw no room to take additional time without injury to my career track. With a due date of November 6, I scheduled my last day for Friday, October 31.

On November 1, feeling something was awry, I rushed to the hospital and was hastened into a terrifying and painful emergency C-section. Once my son was out of the NICU, and we were able to head home, my doctor indicated 10 weeks were needed to recover from the rushed and rugged surgery before I'd be cleared to work. I unsuccessfully pleaded with her to adjust the timeline; my planned six-week absence was already a precarious blemish on my record. After six weeks of so-called leave, I co-wrote and submitted two grant proposals, chaired a graduate student defense, edited two papers for publication, designed and administered several final exams for undergraduate courses with the help of teaching assistants, evaluated student term papers and calculated final grades, and prepared my spring course curriculum, I also took advantage of clichéd doctor handwriting.

Winter break had come to an end and I was prepared and planning to return to the classroom and lab after six weeks of sick leave and an additional week of working remotely during the winter holidays. The secretary of HR had just sent me an email reminding me that their records indicated I was slated to teach several courses in the spring semester and a doctor's note was required to officially return to work. As I packed up my infant son's nap blanket, and bottles, and placed a dozen frozen packets of pumped breast milk in a cooler to send with my son when I dropped him off for his first day in daycare across town, I looked down at my doctor's note. The note listed a date of return well past the start of the semester, another three weeks needed to sufficiently heal, but the handwriting was messy enough that it could conceivably be modified, slightly and undetectably, to permit my return after six weeks. A wave of nausea swelled in me, a confluence of anxiety over the prospect of leaving my infant son in daycare and a cocktail of guilt and frustration at feeling pressed to cross this ethical line, as I gingerly added a few lines to the scrawled date, scanned it, and emailed it to HR. I forged a doctor's note.

Still in pain, my wound insufficiently healed, I strapped ice packs over my stitches with a pregnancy support wrap while I stood before packed classrooms and labs. I exhausted myself micromanaging my schedule to ensure I had 30 minutes to spare every two to three hours, between classes and meetings, trying to avoid the pain and embarrassment of overfull breasts and leaky milk stains on my clothes and to ensure enough milk for my son in daycare the next day. I locked my office door and pumped milk standing at my upright desk while grading exams, editing dissertations, and running statistical analyses to the hum of the breast pump. I thought of how I should be grateful to have a private place to pump. I was subjected to frequent, poorly-veiled, underhanded comments by colleagues about how often my office door was closed. No one asked how I was doing. No one asked about the baby. I was depleted, demoralized, and trying so hard.

Four months later, I stopped at the top of the big stone stairway outside my building, heading out to pick my 4-month-old son up from daycare. I checked to make sure I remembered the hard drive with the data that needed analyzing and my heavy-duty laptop to run the analyses. I was hurrying and anxious, as always at this time of day, driven by heart-racing post-partum anxiety I had been attempting to ignore, amplified by the pressures of work and the visceral craving to be with my son. The day had gone by so quickly. There was still so much work to do. After three miscarriages and so many treatments to try to protect this pregnancy, my son was a miraculous gift. I ached to spend more time with him. I was riddled with guilt for the eight hours he had already spent at daycare and uneasy about the prospect of another near-sleepless night.

Doctors called it colic until we got well past the usual colic months. They reassured me he was eating and growing so everything was fine. The citations and research papers I brought to them, showing what I thought might be wrong, were repeatedly dismissed. I so looked forward to being with my son but dreaded the coming of night and the dawn of another day when I struggled to meet the demands of work and life with so little sleep. Stepping down to the first well-worn grey stone of this big, exposed staircase, my body just shut off. I collapsed downward, tumbling, conscious but without control. When the fall finally stopped itself, I looked around with embarrassment at the handful of concerned onlookers, feebly stood up, and limped away carrying a dented laptop, bruised body, and the weight of more guilt about now being late to pick up my son.

Two months later, joyfully pregnant with my second son, I sat at a tiny table in the office of my department chair. I was flanked by my two mentors, senior faculty members assigned to me when I started, to help guide and support my success on the tenure track. The department chair sat across from me, delivering my annual performance review and ready to discuss my plans and trajectory for the upcoming year. My performance was deemed excellent, with teaching excellence, awards for advising and mentorship under my belt, over $1 million in grants funded, a textbook chapter, and a couple of publications over the last few years. That part of the meeting was cheerful and uneventful.

I took the lead in laying out my plans for the upcoming year. I came armed with lists and targets and timelines and strategies, anxiously hoping to reassure them I would maintain this inhuman level of productivity despite the pending birth of Kiddo #2. My experience in academia before and following the birth of Kid #1 trained me to act as if I was not pregnant, birthing, recovering from a harrowing emergency C-section, or sleepless with a colicky baby. I felt I needed to continue to maintain the appearance of an unflappable, robotically productive, and dependable faculty member solely committed to producing grants and papers with no conflicting commitments.

After this performance of feigned confidence, I was shocked when my male mentor responded to my proposed plan with a lengthy soliloquy about how I should take a full year off because that first year of a child's life is so pivotally important to their development and future, seemingly ignorant to the fact that I had felt all but forced to return to work six weeks after the birth of my first son. Mom's guilt and shame, mixed with confusion and frustration, poured into me as I tried to remain calm and keep my expression unaltered. My female mentor jumped in with a response before I could gather my thoughts.

"That would be the end of her career!" she exclaimed.

She continued, with growing intensity, to say out loud what had previously been unstated but implicitly made clear to me from day one of my first pregnancy. In the hamster wheel-like system of academic productivity, competing for grants, securing funding, acquiring grad students, conducting research, publishing papers, securing more funding to recruit more graduate students to conduct more research to publish more papers ... and there was no room for a pause. Any interruption in this cycle would throw a wrench into the already impossible expectations and the house of cards would come tumbling down. She was saying the things everyone in the progressive academic world refused to admit, and she was right.

There I sat as my two mentors battled it out, watching a living piece of performance art that would have horrified HR, and laid bare the inherent culture of confusion and contradiction about women, mothers, and professional potential that I had been slogging through since my first pregnancy. I just sat there. I said nothing. I attempted to smile and silently watched the clock desperately waiting for the meeting to end.

I've asked myself why I ignored so many red flags until that day I picked up the Mommy Fuel mug, alerting me that something was deeply unsustainable. For goodness' sake, I forged a doctor's note! In 2013, as a postdoctoral researcher on the road to an academic career, I devoured the book "Lean In: Women, Work, and the Will to Lead" by Sheryl Sandberg. I was primed to embrace the case Sandberg made, whole cloth. Born at the tail end of Gen X, I felt utterly free to do, be, or pursue whatever I chose growing up. Firmly accepting the message that permeated the culture, I believed that if I worked hard, being female would be no barrier to my potential success. I trusted that the feminists and progressives before me had not only philosophized about it but had in fact made the world amenable to supporting fully-realized women: as workers, as scholars, as wives and moms. Then I realized that much of what I had believed was a mirage, a phantasm of real hopes, simplistic blue sky thinking, and sophistry.

I leaned in, and I fell down, hard. It took me by surprise, so I searched for a way to make sense of my experience, reading every mommy blog and chat room, every research paper and report. Feeling less alone, I also began to feel angry. When I began my faculty position, the sizable cadre of women in my department, including eight female faculty with tenure, was reassuring. I later realized appearances were not quite what they seemed. According to

2020 U.S. Census data, approximately 16.5% of women over 40 are childless; yet, six of the eight (roughly 75%) tenured female faculty in my department were without children. A cursory swim through the scholarship on women, particularly mothers in academia, was dispiriting. Though estimates vary by academic discipline, Inside Higher Ed reports that studies show women are as much as 55% less likely to get tenure than men. A 2006 study by Ginther and Kahn found that women with children on the tenure track are much more likely to drop off the tenure track than men or women without children and concluded that the gap in promotion and tenure is entirely explained by what they call "fertility decisions"– motherhood. Not surprisingly the American Association of University Women reports that in the US, approximately 70% of male professors with tenure have children compared to only 44% of female tenured professors. And that's just the tip of the iceberg of literature. Representation largely comprised of women without children can hardly be said to be representative of women. Why had so many of us been let down, even betrayed, by our culture and our institutions in this way?

12

GUARDED

MARY C. GILLEN

It was 1955, and I was ecstatic when I learned there was a girls' basketball team at my Catholic high school in the Bronx. I loved basketball even though, at 13, I had held a ball just once until the boys at the playground grabbed it from me.

In my sophomore year, I tried out for St. Helena's junior varsity team. I was eliminated after the first round.

A month later, curly-haired Kathleen Martin transferred from a public school into my class. On her second day, she announced that she had permission to try out for—not the junior varsity—but the varsity.

"I will make the team! But I need to find the gym."

"I'll take you to the gym!" I offered. "I have to go there anyway." I had to fib—this seemed like a chance to be on the team.

After school, dressed in our knee-length, heavy cotton gym uniforms, we strutted from the girls building across the dirt parking lot to the red brick boys' gym, opened the sagging double doors, and marched into the dust-smelly gym. We were late. The girls had started their practice. Kathleen scanned the area. I followed her when she strode over to the end of a fast-moving group of varsity players who were passing, dribbling, and shooting too fast for me to keep up. I stepped out of the line, gasping, my heart pounding.

I watched Kathleen. She was amazing. She passed behind her back. Dribbled through and around her legs. Took hook shots, jump shots. Rebounded like a kangaroo. Oh Yeah! Kathleen definitely belonged with the best players.

My future best friend, Betty, a pretty redhead, rescued me. She tugged on my gym suit, then pulled me over to the junior varsity line and slid in behind me.

"Stay here with the guards so you don't have to shoot" she said. "Follow the girl in front of you."

I nodded!

"Rebound...take two bounces then pass the ball – over the center line to the forwards."

I followed Betty's instructions, copying the girl in front of me.

I had no clue that I was on the defensive side of the court. Yup! Until 1968, and the ratification by Congress of Title IX, defensive and offensive players were restricted to the six-player half of the court game.

"One of you two new girls does not belong here!" shouted Miss Finneran, the coach. "Please leave!"

If I had left, I would have felt like the ball was snatched from me, again. But what if this new girl told on me? Kathleen and I looked at each other. She just shrugged and kept playing.

I ignored Miss Finneran, dribbling and passing those musty-smelling, near-bald basketballs, donated to the girls' team when the boys' team was finished with them.

"Coach is a softie," Betty whispered. "She'll probably let you play with the JV."

And she did!

Miss Finneran went through a bag of discarded uniforms. She pulled out a one-piece-too-large-holey-gray-white uniform. I loved it! It was perfect!

There was more to being on that team, more than loving the game of basketball. It was a journey of discovery; of an awareness of why, from first grade on, I was attracted to girls, particularly redheaded girls. The support of Miss Finneran, another redhead, and the athletic girls on my team gave me, for the first time in my life, a place to breathe; a place where I could pull off part of the mask I didn't know I was wearing.

After several days, I had the courage to tell my parents that I was on the team, terrified they would forbid me from playing. I was 15. Their supportive attitude toward my interest in sports had diminished. With puberty came a set of expectations from my neighborhood friends that I could neither meet nor want to meet.

My announcement to Mom and Dad was met with silence, then with questions: "Why didn't you ask permission? Where did you learn to play basketball? Who is this coach? Is she one of the nuns?" And, from Dad, "Maybe we shouldn't let you play basketball!"

"My two sisters and I played on the basketball team at my high school... around 1915," Mom said. "We had to wear bloomers!" Then she laughed, easing the tension in the room.

I showed them my beloved uniform. Dad sat still, frowning; I was sure he wouldn't let me play. He stood up and left the room, shaking his head. I took a deep breath. Mom had opened the way for me.

"I'll give your decrepit piece of cloth a good washing with bleach! I doubt anything will help it, ever!"

One afternoon following lunch, I returned to my unusually noisy classroom.

"Mary, did you hear about Patty and Delores? I hadn't.

"They've been suspended for being lesbians."

"What's a lesbian?"

"Girls who love each other. Sister caught them making out in the bathroom.

At first, my heart soared with joy! There were words for what I was experiencing. I wasn't the only one in the world who liked girls. My new feeling of normalcy, of happiness was jolted when I realized that Patty and Delores were punished. Worse, classmates said that Patty and Delores were sinners, destined for hell.

I knew I would be in trouble if I wasn't careful to hide what I felt.

Junior-year basketball was filled with league games, tournament championships, and camaraderie. I inherited the graduating team captain's pristine uniform. Betty was elected JV co-captain. Kathleen disappeared by the end of junior year. Perhaps her family moved again. I missed her as a friend and teammate.

That year, I read the American Psychiatric Association's 1955 definition of homosexuality. It contained words like mentally ill, defective, and degenerate. I was shocked and confused. I wasn't any of those things—was I? Yes, everyone, especially my family, would see me as defensive and sick.

That definition haunted and destroyed many lives. Those condemning words remained part of the psychiatric classification of homosexuality until 1973.

For the remainder of high school, basketball and softball doubled in importance. I was known as a capable athlete and a fun person. At home and in my neighborhood I was an oddity. Comments were made by neighbors and my father, who indicated that I was not trying to be a normal young woman. I realized that it wasn't enough to be careful about what I said. I had to live a secret life. Gay today! Straight tomorrow!

In 1967, nine years after graduating from St. Helena's, I returned as head Physical Education teacher and varsity coach. At that time, Catholic schools could and did hire uncertified teachers—someone like me who was working part-time toward a degree. I submitted my application with my transcript listing a limited number of credits from Queens College, extolled my experience playing on numerous teams, and emphasized my varsity years at St. Helena's. I wanted that job! A new gymnasium was built just for the girls!

During the interview, I was exuberant and attentive. I thought I had charmed the principal Sister Elizabeth, because she immediately and with enthusiasm offered me the position.

"Mary, I'm thrilled you'll be teaching with us! Your aunt, Sr. Catherine, was my French teacher and mentor. She was extraordinary! I'm sure you're just like her!"

Others' expectations of me to be a mirror image of my aunt had followed me throughout high school. I was determined that this would not happen again! At 27, I thought this comparison to my aunt, who died 20 years earlier, whom I loved, would have ended.

My two years at St. Helena's took my life in a more productive direction. It was the late 60s. The civil rights movement was having a positive impact on behalf of African Americans. The Women's Liberation Movement began to expand the rights of women. The gay community joined their momentum. Women—lesbians and straight—envisioned playing sports as talented athletes without slurs or objects thrown at them. LGBT people deserved to socialize at a gay bar or restaurant without being terrorized or arrested. We were fed up with living our lives in the shadows.

I was emboldened by this progress for women and as part of the LGBT community. This enabled me to hold my own as a respected member of the teaching staff. I was no longer just Sister Catherine's niece. I was a person with my own strengths and abilities.

Despite my new courage, society's rejection of gays and being in a Catholic environment weighed heavily on me. I was terrified someone would "out" me. Dating a woman was exciting, yet risky. Like most lesbians, I tried to date guys while secretly dating women. To hide our lives from co-workers, we invented a social life consisting of straight male and female friends. It was exhausting!

I partied too much, and worried about becoming an alcoholic. I destroyed all photographs of myself and my lesbian friends. My internalized homophobia led me to distance myself from my straight friends and my family. Betty and I stayed connected until she entered the convent. Betty was committed to the teachings of the Catholic Church. Perhaps she might tell me that I was damned for eternity. Suppose this were true?

Our high school basketball team won a CYO championship in 1968 and placed second in 1969.

Shortly before the 1968 game, my father died not understanding yet loving his unorthodox daughter.

The girls still played the outdated two-section, half-court offensive-defensive game. Mom thought this was an improvement over the three-section court game she played in 1915. But not enough.

These rules for high school and college sports were governed by the National Division of Women's and Girls Sports (DWGS)—ironically created and enforced by female physical education professionals and colleagues who believed that we were too frail to withstand hard exercise. Playing men's/boys' rules was unladylike, making us masculine. I was stifled and angry with these restrictions, both as a player and as a coach. The demeaning rules were emotionally and psychologically harmful to females. These "guidelines" were also supported by male administrators to keep women "in their place" and to prevent us from becoming a threat to their egos.

Prior to and while coaching at St. Helena's, I played full-court five-player basketball with a team from the Industrial League and an Amateur Athletic Union (AAU) team, the Merry Mixers. This was a team I formed, named, and briefly coached. However, I was restless. I saw women basketball players who had a higher caliber of skills, strategy, and education. Their daily lives had more purpose and more orientation to long-term goals. I heard stories about The All American Red Heads.[1] These extraordinary athletes, advocates in sneakers and shorts, barnstormed the country challenging and changing outdated ideas about women's physical capabilities.

I had to absorb this energy. Lucille Kyvallos, a trailblazer for women's scholastic and collegiate basketball, was hired to coach the Queen's College women's basketball team. I left St. Helena's in 1969 to attend Queens College full-time and continued as a manager for her team. Coach Kyvallos served on the boards of the U. S. Olympic Regional Committee for six years and the DWGS to push for change in women's basketball.

By 1970, most secondary and collegiate schools, including Queens College, played the faster-paced, more challenging, and exciting five-player full-court game. As one of Coach Kyvallos' managers and an experienced player, I had a great time filling in for practice and scrimmages.

Coach Kyvallos displayed her confidence in each of us as strong, capable women who could and should strive to meet our potential,

---

1. Molina, John, BARNSTORMING AMERICA: Stories from the Pioneers of Women's Basketball, Acclaim Press, 2016.

to be efficient, proficient, and professional. She encouraged us to embrace the Queens College mission: to serve as innovative leaders in a diverse world that they make more equitable and inclusive.

The Merry Mixers merged with the Chuckles to form a semi-professional team called Planters Peanuts. I heard that some of these players were recruited by the newly formed professional WBL (Women's Basketball League).

The crowning jewel was February 22, 1975. Queens College played and won the first-ever women's basketball game held at Madison Square Garden.[2]

Now at 83 years of age, I see my skinny 13-year-old self, hugging a basketball. Hungry to play.

Thanks, boys. For a gift; a wake-up call. A knowing that I would play basketball. And that I would be who I am.

---

2. Hult, Joan S. & Marianna Trekell, A Century of Women's Basketball: From Frailty to Final Four, American Alliance for Health, Physical Education, Recreation and Dance 1991. Madison Square Garden, pp. 360 - 361.

13

WIDENING THE CIRCLE: REFLECTIONS ON INCLUSIVE WITCHERY

SANDY GREENBERG

In the Ghoul-haunted Woodland of Weir

As shadows lengthen, the harvest moon creeps into view.

On most days, I feel powerless. The world is impossibly cruel and impossibly broken. More often than not, we are unable to fully atone for our own transgressions, let alone to care for those afflicted by deeper injustices. Ours is a bureaucratic world; again and again, institutional avenues for change seem woefully inadequate, but we have nowhere else to turn. It is all I can do to force myself, however much I can, to bear witness. To pay attention; to care. Bearing witness is important, but is hardly a tonic for powerlessness.

With the coming of autumn, however, something changes. Fall is a time of harvest plenty and a time of incipient gloom. Fall is a time of coming together and of death. Fall is a borderland; uncanny and uncertain and unbounded. Fall is a time of indistinct forces, stirring within. In the fall, the world seems imbued with power.

I don't think I am alone in this. Of the season, John Clare wrote,[1] *"Whoever looks round sees Eternity there."* Edgar Allan Poe's enigmatic *Ulalume* [2] is set on a *"night in the lonesome October"* in the *"ghoul-haunted woodland of Weir." Ulalume* is the tale of a strange, mystical rendezvous; an eerie stroll taken through realms of ancient deities and departed souls. As a narrative, it's hopelessly opaque. Still, I like to think Poe and I are in agreement: in the fall, the line dividing the natural from the supernatural seems to grow blurred. As the veil thins, powerlessness dissipates. Within me, there arises a new sensation: power.

Zing, Zing, Zing!

My ruminations on power eventually delivered me, of course, to the occult. Witchcraft – the art of harnessing supernatural energies to secure particular ends – seems almost synonymous with power. In contrast, contemporary Western spirituality seems to locate power somewhere just out of reach. References to "a higher power" are taken as inoffensive religiously neutral language. The underlying assumption is that whatever religious doctrine you profess, its locus of power lies somewhere external, somewhere greater-than.

That most of us find such nebulous language agreeable, or at least tolerable, speaks to how distant this "higher power" has come to seem. Within the cultural mainstream, when believers describe God as a source of "strength" in their lives they are usually gesturing towards mental or emotional fortitude. "Power," on the other hand,

---

1. https://www.poetryfoundation.org/poems/43946/autumn-56d222d7e0f7c

2. https://poets.org/poem/ulalume

invokes the all-encompassing sovereignty held by God alone. God may attend to requests made in prayer but seems unlikely to bestow supernatural "powers" on a human supplicant.

Western religion was not always thus. Classical religion was explicitly contractual, an orientation summed up in the Latin formula *do ut des*,[3] meaning "I give that you might give." For as long as the proper sacrifices were carried out, the gods would provide tangible services in return. Although the gods ultimately effectuated these boons, the system's regularity gave great influence to ritual specialists. Proper ritual depended on the expertise of priests and priestesses; supernatural beneficence depended on proper ritual. These women and men could rightly be said to wield supernatural power – and, concomitantly, social and political power.

Neither ancient Christianity nor early Islam strayed too far from this framework. Adherents' day-to-day life abounded with amulets, charms, incantations, and minor rituals,[4] all of which possessed magical efficacy. Whether employed by clerics or commoners, magic served practical ends: warding off disease, garnering wealth, and the like. What sounds to us like witchcraft was once ubiquitous.

The magic of yore is never quite forgotten. From time to time, one comes across ritual practices that hint at a distant lineage. Separated from the classical world by a thousand years and several thousand miles, a 19th-century Amish grimoire[5] provides all manner

---

3. https://www.patheos.com/blogs/bythepalemoonlight/2020/11/pax-deorum-the
-formula-of-do-ut-des-making-of-offerings/

4. https://www.coptic-magic.phil.uni-wuerzburg.de/

5. http://www.cunning.org.uk/powwow.pdf?fbclid=IwAR3zJZJUW6lZ_-XiH1T2
vuG7VEbHQtZHEuezMB82M7nAqzHBdJzygRJPxyE

of spells and incantations. To heal yourself from snakebite, you are instructed to recite:

> *God has created all things and they were good;*
> *Thou only, serpent, art damned,*
> *Cursed be thou and thy sting.*
> [here make the sign of the cross three times before concluding]
> *Zing, zing, zing!*

Less overtly, plenty of 21st-century Catholics still recite a rhyming couplet calling upon St. Anthony's help to recover misplaced objects. It's difficult to know what to call this practice if not a spell.

Nevertheless, ritual magic has been pushed far away from the core experience of Western devotional life. It's well worth speculating as to how this happened. Perhaps, as society at large has become increasingly secular, the function of religion has become increasingly therapeutic. For many of us, living in a religiously diverse and strongly rationalist environment, the supernatural offers comforting reprieve, but rarely actionable guidance—let alone ritual potency. Or perhaps the notion that *we* might be able to channel mystic forces has been worn away by centuries of relentless emphasis on Grace, the theological insistence that salvation is bestowed, rather than earned. Even Pentecostals and Charismatics,[6] contemporary denominations with robust theologies of direct intervention, generally speak of *receiving* gifts of the Spirit, rather than of human agency in reaching for these blessings.

---

6. https://www.bbc.co.uk/religion/religions/christianity/subdivisions/pentecostal_1 .shtml

For my money, though, the marginalization of ritual power was above all else a political project. Medieval Scholastics [7] did not deny magic's efficacy. Instead, following Augustine, they tended to argue that sorcery relied on the intermediary work of demons. Necromantic rituals "worked" by enlisting demonic assistance and—whether or not the necromancer knew it—ultimately securing the necromancer's damnation. Such rituals were to be avoided not because they were powerless, but because they represented a choice to side with Satan and against the Church. In practice, this worldview precipitated centuries of clerical efforts to concentrate metaphysical power in the Church (which was, of course, a political as well as a spiritual entity). Once ubiquitous forms of folk magic were increasingly targeted by the ecclesiastical apparatus. The clerics' dragnets did not spare those who described their occultism in explicitly Christian terms—to take a particularly colorful example, Thiess of Kaltenbrun,[8] who described himself as a werewolf in the service of Christ. The Church—and, later, the Churches—strove not to abolish magic, but to monopolize it.

And so the non-clerical magic of daily life was pushed to the fringes, if never quite eliminated. This was a political watershed as much as a religious one. "Providence" may justify the existing order. "Salvation" may inspire efforts to challenge it. Magic puts the power in *your* hands, in everyone's hands, forcing us to choose how we are to use it. Magic is political, and therein lies its danger—but also its promise.

---

7. https://www.youtube.com/watch?v=MI3Q2ShVKJY

8. https://en.wikipedia.org/wiki/Thiess_of_Kaltenbrun

The institutional means by which we are directed to make our voices heard tend to feel lifeless and sterile. Witchcraft conjures an image of power that can transcend institutional gatekeepers. Occultic power feels immediate, even sensual. In 2020, witches across the United States started coming out of the woodwork to hex Donald Trump's reelection bid. It was a telling moment.

Western occultism is today decentralized and strongly anti-establishment in character. Unsurprisingly so. Over the centuries, the dominant institutions rejected witchcraft. The witches, in turn, rejected the institutions. As ever, those who feel themselves excluded from institutions of power continue to seek out countercultural reservoirs of power: it is no surprise that across the Western world, most users of ritual magic are women.

To be clear, no one is suggesting that those of us driven to fight injustice should spend our time casting hexes *instead of* voting. Even occultists can walk and chew gum. Still, in the ghoul-haunted, magic-infused woodlands of autumn, I do not feel quite so powerless against the world's ills. Today's witchcraft answers a common and desperate need—the need for an experience of power.

Open Sesame!

One way to feel powerful is to exclude others.

The panoply of religious systems in which individuals are said to possess magical faculties have always differed widely on how those faculties come to be. In West African Vodun,[9] kinship and lineage are essential determinants of which practitioners can exercise which

---

9. https://en.wikipedia.org/wiki/West_African_Vodun

powers. In Gardnerian Wicca[10], magical competencies are available to anyone, albeit only attainable after difficult study and formal ordination. Today's occultism is eclectic and decentralized, but exclusivist attitudes are not uncommon. Scrolling through social media, it is easy to find people claiming that any number of events in their lives—sightings of black cats, eye contact made with infants, and other perfectly banal happenings—are, in fact, augurs of the witchy prowess with which they, unlike most, were born.

If you have experienced exclusion, the impulse to reciprocate is natural. Among witches, claims of distinct occultic gifts are usually more or less benign. At their most extreme iterations, though, you will run into occultists whose practice seems almost defined by exclusion. Certain currents within Dianic Witchcraft,[11] a tradition oriented around the divinity of womanhood, are deeply hostile to transgender people. Other occultists, influenced by Madame Blavatsky,[12] still cling to her racist (and race-exclusionary) beliefs.

In truth, such occultists are profoundly mistaken. While there is indeed power in keeping others out, there is yet *more* power in *letting others in.*

Witchcraft is political. Witchcraft *must* be political. Witchcraft channels cosmic power through the marginalized, the displaced. Witchcraft channels power through *us*. Because of this, witchcraft was pushed out of the cultural mainstream. Because of this, witchcraft reemerges in times of shared helplessness. The world at large is built on exclusion, on a tightly wound lattice of oppressive systems

---

10. https://en.wikipedia.org/wiki/Gardnerian_Wicca

11. https://en.wikipedia.org/wiki/Dianic_Wicca

12. https://en.wikipedia.org/wiki/Helena_Blavatsky

by which some are said to matter less than others. If witchcraft is to remain subversive, in any way, it must be different.

Radical inclusion is, in and of itself, a strange and forbidden magic. As I write this, the world is cold and damp. Wet leaves plaster the ground. I remember *Ulalume*; here too the skies are *"ashen and sober."* I am at once mighty and powerless. I am the October skies, I am the waterlogged earth, I am sleek and I am ravishing. I am a witch, and I must use my craft for the good. I am a witch, and I must extend the unbroken circle. I am a witch, and I *must*—I can feel it in my bones—I must throw open the door in welcome.

14

A Neighborhood for Children

Samuel D. Gruber

My children grew up in our Syracuse streetcar suburb, known as the Westcott Neighborhood, named after its main street. We never had a chance to ride the streetcar line around which this neighborhood was built. The last car ran more than 80 years ago, but the shape of the neighborhood still reflects its origins. Westcott was built before everyone needed a car, and when they had a car, they did not need it to go everywhere in their daily lives.

Our houses are close together, the blocks are laid out in a mostly orderly fashion, and it is still easy to know one's neighbors. We walk to the library, playgrounds, and parks. In past decades, residents could walk to local stores for most everyday needs. For more excitement and options until 1941, when the streetcar stopped running, they would hop one downtown to work, shopping, or recreation. A century later, the neighborhood still provides just the right amount of space and security mixed with room to roam and places for adventure. We have postage-stamp front lawns, but when viewed together, they seem like a village common. There still is a short but vital commercial strip, though the drugstore and hardware store have left, and it is now filled mostly with eateries. Connecting sidewalks keep us moving around the block and from place to place much like the conveyor belt in the local sushi restaurant. They tie all properties together like neat ribbons around a lovely package. These days, those ribbons still work but are a bit tattered. Best not to look at your phone while walking, you might trip where an old tree root has heaved the pavement upward an inch or more.

Where I began my childhood in the suburbs of Philadelphia, the sidewalks were not so important. Every house had an ample front and backyard and a paved driveway. When we kids needed to get from one house to another we just cut across lawns. When my family uprooted and moved to a brownstone rowhouse in Center City Philadelphia this all changed. In the city, there was no yard to speak of, just a small dark fenced space behind the house accessible only through our gloomy basement, and that opened onto an alley behind a dark looming church. Instead, the front stoop and the sidewalk were our gathering spot and play area for stoopball, half-ball, and team freeze tag. Sometimes when there were enough of us, we'd just take over a block of 22nd Street to play touch football. There were too many of us to run over, so the cars would have to wait. It was a mostly unsupervised childhood that granted independence, but as we grew older, that came with danger, too.

Westcott, where I have lived in the same house for 30 years, is a line (not the only line) where city and suburb meet. This is true for most streetcar suburbs nationwide. Our children learn the neighborhood textures and moods incrementally and when they reach the age of ten or so, their awareness grows exponentially. Each stage of life from infancy through high school exposes them to more and more places and allows them to interact with many more people, and individuals of all types.

Parents acclimate their young to the neighborhood in much the same way I've been watching a robin on my windowsill fledge its young. It's a step-by-step process that for the robin takes just a week or so, but for humans takes years. I went through this process with my children, and I see it repeated year after year with new neighborhood babies with little change. First, a new parent walks past my house with the baby in a snuggly, and then perhaps in a baby carriage, and then a stroller. Soon parents and child are walking around the block hand in hand. In no time toddlers chug ahead—and look back. There is always the suspense of whether will they fall forward on the shallow slopes of the sidewalks or right themselves in time. In winter these same sidewalk swells, rising and falling on the shallow hills, became the first slopes for sledding for the under-three set.

Children learn to bike ride on sidewalks and their first forays away from home are often solo rides (on the sidewalk) around the block. Soon they are on their own, or with friends, circling the block, not seeing the parents—who still are keeping a watchful eye. A little later some children will walk to school (while late sleepers are driven by their parents). The distance to the neighborhood school defines the limit of a child's neighborhood. Friends might be scattered anywhere along the way. This is a familiar distance they can walk if they must, and they know all the different routes and how long they take. They learn how to hurry and how to dawdle, and in so doing they learn unconsciously the difference between long blocks and short blocks, flat streets and hilly streets, and maybe as a life lesson—when to work hard and when to slack off.

Children practice telling stories, spending money, and making choices as they wander by the neighborhood's houses and in our little business district. Their imaginations transform the ordinary and the everyday—those things we often take for granted. For the young, these things are new and challenging. With good balance, you can walk on the curb, which other times is the mouse's sidewalk.

Adults, with their deep memories, like to imagine there are ghosts in old houses. Children experience enchantment. They are still fresh in a world where everything, no matter its history, is equally new. The more varied a neighborhood's shapes, colors, sizes, textures, smells, and sounds, then the greater the enchantment and stimulus for creative imagining. My daughter and her best friend imagined the big maple on the grassy berm in front of our house as a fairy tree. They knew instinctively that this was a liminal space. They'd sit there for hours telling stories and serving tea, and they'd leave all kinds of objects as offerings. The ancient Greeks believed there were dryads in trees, and nature spirits that could take the form of a beautiful young woman. I'm not sure what the girls believed about the tree, but I think they imagined families of fairies living in its thick trunk or in its full canopy, where I saw and heard only nattering squirrels.

The young experience neighborhoods differently than adults. Some of these differences are visible and some are not. They travel at a different pace and a different height. Small children are closer to the ground and their eyesight is good. When walking is still new, they look down more than up. They find bugs on the sidewalk and fat worms after the rain. One year I emptied the small colored stones from a fish tank onto my desiccated driveway to fill some of the cracks and holes. Though hardly visible to a standing or striding adult's eyes, those stones were magical magnets for the toddlers on my street. They had to stop and find them. The little pebbles were more valuable than diamonds.

For a child, small things are enough. Each is a part of their world-building. Variety—especially without undue anxiety—is more than the spice of life, it is a yeast that makes it rise. Adults can be transported, too, though it might take more stimuli. The first crocuses and daffodils on a warm day of spring, or a blaze of red maple leaves in October are dramatic and restorative.

Children go barefoot in summer whenever they can. They know the feel of soft wet grass, the jab of a twig or sharp plant stem on a tenderfoot, and the textures and temperature of concrete, whether cool and smooth or hot as a frying pan. Concrete is non-violent, but it defends itself as many scraped knees and elbows attest. Kids ignore the buildup of grime on the bottoms of their feet. They know the smell of flowers and the itch of poison ivy. Their fiercest competitors are the neighborhood dogs, which they encounter face-to-face. My dog is gentle with little children but wants to push her long snout into their faces. Kids may see cats sunning on porches or in driveways, but cats avoid those sticky hands.

In both suburbs and the city, sidewalks are used for hopscotch. Since the advent of colored chalk, sidewalks have become a veritable art room for children (and some adults) with bright pictures and patterns in front of many houses. In the spring especially, when the snow and ice have melted and good weather has returned, the young artists get to work. As I walk around the block the prevalence of chalk art is a good indication of the demographic health of our neighborhood.

Children are active—with permission or not. They face neighborhood boundaries that are insignificant or unnoticed by their elders. They'll trailblaze where grown-ups never think to tread. Children discover the world by moving beyond their rooms, from their houses, and their streets. They squeeze through hedges, and duck under chains, ropes, and even crime scene tape. For many of my boyhood friends, barriers were a challenge to be met, not an imposition.

There are secret paths, favorite trees, and walls, and plenty of places to avoid. There are houses to head for and some to steer clear of.

Sidewalks are the hallways of a neighborhood where people encounter each other and choose to engage or avoid. Front yards—when they exist—are public rooms off the hallways. Backyards are more private. Sidewalks also frame the block. They set limits and suggest rules. Young adolescents, often fearless of retribution, will trespass across yards and soon slide between houses, around fences, and move from street to street across the blocks instead of around them. To tell city children to "stay in the backyard" is like sending them to their room, literally grounding them in one small rectangular property parcel. There are things to do in a bedroom and the backyard, but many fewer adventures there, and very little risk.

As spring progresses and the days get longer, kids are out later, until in summer the older ones are running around or on their bikes and scooters until it is almost dark. Teenagers play ball in the street. But like some endangered species, the numbers of children have been plummeting in my neighborhood. Family houses have been turned into student rentals, and the habitat for children is much diminished. On some city streets, one is more likely to sight a deer than a child. Even those houses that are owner-occupied or are rented to non-students have few kids. There is an aging population of empty-nesters (I am one) and couples without children, complemented by the young and hip who have postponed and sometimes renounced starting new families entirely. But that might change. There are ebbs and flows in the local demographics. I've recently counted at least a dozen children still at home on just two long blocks of Allen Street, a notable uptick for a street once full of them.

In time, our children leave the neighborhood and even the town and state. They go off to college, go off to war, and off to romance and adventure. We are grateful to our neighbors, and the physical neighborhood itself, for the street smarts our children acquire along the way. Someday I hope there will be an active family in my house again – but not too soon. I'm content still living here, to experience the seasons changing, listening for the shouts of children.

15

LITTLE WOMEN GONE ROGUE

FELICIA HAURY

On the surface, a stranger would see two innocent Black schoolgirls on a typical walk home from school. In September 1971, my cousin Lydia and I were six years old and entrusted with the task of making it to the babysitter's house alone after school. We were in the first grade on the first day of school three blocks away from Lydia's house. Our first feat was to cross the main street at the traffic light. I recall the terror of watching the speeding cars swish by in both directions. We stood uncomfortable in the still lingering summer heat of a Los Angeles afternoon waiting for the light to turn green. School paperwork was pinned to the front of our white starched Peter Pan blouses and plaid jumpers. My stiff new saddle shoes hurt my toes and I could feel the nickel working its way to my heels. I kept leaning over to scratch behind the elastic tops of my knee-high socks that were cutting off my circulation. To honor the first day of school, the night before, our aunt Red had expertly straightened our hair with a hot comb and put it in two curled pigtails, then, cut us bangs that were now pasted to our foreheads. I remember wanting to look like Cindy from The Brady Bunch. Following the crowd, we managed to reach the other side of the street unscathed.

Lydia and I were destined playmates. Our mothers were sisters who were pregnant with us at the same time. I was born in April and Lydia in July. Our mothers even had the rhyming names Earline and Verline. Despite our similarities, Lydia and I had vastly different personalities. She was daring and brave while I was timid and cautious. Lydia had butterscotch skin to my cocoa brown. She preferred black licorice while I loved red licorice. We both had older sisters who couldn't be bothered with us. Lydia was adventurous and would get irritated when I curled up with books to the point where she would rip them from my hands to make me play outside with her. She was also competitive and became furious if I beat her at Checkers or Monopoly. She preferred hopscotch where she beat me every time.

The babysitter's house sat on the corner down the street from Lydia's house. After our adventure of crossing the main street, we went to the store on the other side that sold penny candy. At the front of the store were baskets with sheets of candy buttons, bubble gum, and chocolate that sat underneath the cash register. I retrieved the nickel I had been saving in my shoe all day to purchase five pieces of carefully selected candies. Savoring the treats we went on to the next block and stood in line with a group of neighborhood children waiting to enter Ms. Betty's home. Although small, we were the last ones in line. We peered around the other children and saw that Ms. Betty was a big stern woman threatening to spank anyone who misbehaved. The other children seemed afraid of her. Lydia and I exchanged indignant glances questioning why we needed to go to a babysitter in the first place, pioneers as we were with free-range parenting. As we moved closer to Ms. Betty's door, Lydia and I became increasingly frightened. Once Ms. Betty turned her head, Lydia grabbed my arm and said, "Let's go!" She didn't have to tell me twice.

I should have known leaving the babysitters would lead to trouble based on a vivid recent memory. While playing outside Lydia's house, she convinced me to follow her to the church rectory a block away. I asked, "What for?" She didn't answer and just pulled me along. The side door was unlocked as churches tended to be in those days. Lydia put her index finger to her lips imploring me to be quiet. It was cool and silent inside as we walked up a narrow stairway to the second floor. I followed her into a small classroom. She seemed to know where she was going and what she wanted. I watched puzzled as she quietly opened a closet door and dragged out a large blue plastic bag filled with popped popcorn. I surmised this was her Sunday school classroom and the popcorn was a snack issued by the nuns. Eyes wide open I shook my head *No* but Lydia pushed past me with the three-foot bag of popcorn bouncing down the stairs behind her. As I said a silent prayer in my head asking God for forgiveness I heard footsteps in the hallway. I stumbled down the stairs and hurried behind Lydia as we both ran down the street as fast as we could with the bounty.

Later that evening, our mothers found out we were missing when attempting to retrieve us from Ms. Betty's house. My mother worked as a grocery clerk and Lydia's mother was a nurse. According to my aunt, Ms. Betty was hysterical. After canvassing the neighborhood our parents came to the house to regroup. They discovered me and Lydia on the floor eating snacks and watching television. I remember the anger and shouts of "Why didn't you go to Ms. Betty's like I told you?!" Getting a whooping was a real danger in those days and as my aunt came near me wielding a belt I retreated to the bed screaming before she even touched me to the point where she lowered her arm and started laughing. Lydia was clearly tougher than me and had braced herself to take her licks with dignity. I don't recall my mother punishing me. I guess she was just glad I was safe.

It wasn't the end of the world like another taboo we challenged the previous spring. At church, I was forbidden to take what I now know as communion in the Catholic Church. My parents were not especially religious, and I had spotty attendance at both Baptist and Catholic Churches. Lydia, on the other hand, had just completed her first communion. I was secretly jealous when she got to wear what looked to me like a miniature-sized wedding dress and veil. The priest was an old white gentleman who stood at a corner podium speaking what I now know was Latin. I watched enviously as Lydia was able to go up that day and have the body of Christ placed in her mouth. She walked piously back to our pew and knelt beside me. I whispered, "How does it taste?" Lydia discreetly removed part of the wafer from her mouth and placed the disintegrating disc in my mouth. Mystery solved. We didn't go straight to hell as the adults would have us believe.

I imagine our mothers as two young girls braving the world together much like Lydia and me. Recently, I heard a story of how Lydia's mother, Aunt Earline, was like the alarm clock for them on school days. She could be counted on to get them up no matter how late my mother stayed up, which she did often. They attended Catholic school and Earline aspired to be a nun. My mother, on the other hand, had to be frequently redirected. She liked to read fashion and gossip magazines, buy the latest records, and talk to boys. They did not have a hands-on mother yet managed to make it through their childhood as two strong women. Lydia and I unwittingly followed in their footsteps. Forging independence with our divergent temperaments at a time when children were less monitored.

I started off as a timid little girl and became stronger having passed this threshold of independence. Most of the choices were guided by Lydia but they were made without adult supervision. We both asserted ourselves as individuals. These traits have followed us throughout our lives paralleling the similarities we have with our mothers as sisters. Lydia and I now live on opposite sides of the country. I'm still in California and she is in Maryland. We squeezed one or two more adventures in during our teen years like necking in cars with boys but nothing as exceptional as running away from the babysitter. Nowadays we are approaching retirement and complaining about the aches and pains of getting older. We laugh at the modern concepts of free range and helicopter parenting, or "it takes a village to raise a child." We know a parent's gaze can go only so far.

Our escape from Ms. Betty's has become a family legend, told at gatherings whenever anyone wants to emphasize or poke fun at the difference between my and Lydia's personalities and our exploits as children. My Aunt Earline says that Lydia and I were switched at birth because I tend to act more like her, reserved and disciplined, while Lydia behaves more like my mother, outgoing and talkative. My mother gets angry when she hears this and tells her sister, "You got the right one."

16

HUMILIATION

KAREN HEMPSON

Plunging into the pool, I heard the late bell ring while in midair. The coach shot me a disdainful look. Clasping her clipboard with a whistle around her neck, and sweatshirt over a bathing suit, she sneered, "That was a close one, Karen. You just made it."

Miss Decker flaunted her intolerance for struggling swimmers like me. It was not that I did not try. I was not good enough. In Coach's world, it did not matter that I maintained a high academic average. She adhered strictly to the rule that if one passes all rigorous swimming tests, she may be excused in her senior year from swim class. I failed the last part of the test.

I successfully demonstrated the backstroke, sidestroke, butter-fly, and breaststrokes, even treading water for ten minutes without touching the pool's sides or bottom. Failing to rescue a "drowning" swimmer sealed my doom.

To demonstrate a rescue, I jumped into the three-foot shallow end and swam to the eight-foot section where a tall student waited. I gently grabbed her, turned her around while placing my arm across her chest, and delivered her back to the shallow end. My five-foot stature made it difficult to lock her in place while swimming, so she technically "drowned." The punitive sentence of enduring my senior year with forty weeks of swim class interfered with my demanding academic schedule, part-time job, and college admissions applications.

Miss Decker showed no empathy, nor did she remediate my shortcomings. In retrospect, I wish I was given more instruction and practice if ever I had to save a future swimmer. That would have made my time valuable.

"Okay, everyone, warm up with laps," Coach bellowed. Her words echoed throughout the high-ceilinged pool arena; her brash demeanor was accentuated by a hoarse, raspy voice. I synchronized with swimmers in my roped-off line, alternating between sidestroke and backstroke.

After fifteen minutes, the whistle blew for the class to gather around two diving boards. The low board was used for practice diving and novices like myself. Advanced swimmers were allowed to use the high diving board.

"Listen up. Today, we will learn back flips. You may not get this at first, but don't be afraid to try. Jim, please come forward."

A bean-pole with gangly arms and hollowed abdomen mounted the board in a Speedo and waited for Miss Decker's instructions, "Stand at the end of the board, your back to the pool, heels hanging off the board. To get a good spring, jump from your toes with arms in the air, arching your back. Then grab your knees to your chest and transfer all your weight in front of your body to complete the flip. Forgetting to arch your back will result in a painful belly or back flop."

On command, Jim sprang off into a backward body circle, then completed his dive like a swan, head first, feet barely making a splash.

"Nice job. Jim won a medal for this technique on the swim team. Any questions?"

Students stood like statues, staring in disbelief. Coach quickly scanned our group for questions. When no one raised a hand, she ordered, "Line up."

"I'll never need to know how to dive backward," I protested to Judy, another senior sentenced to this class.

She whispered, "I can't do this. I don't want to do this. I should have told her I have my monthly."

The "warden" meticulously recorded our monthly periods on her clipboard to catch any girl falsely claiming an extra period to get out of class. She suspected all excuses as deceitful. Coach, however, released my older sister from senior year swimming after she contacted ringworm.

What luck.

Judy continued, "Remember how Ted fell off the high-dive practicing that flip?"

"Yeah, that's what I'm afraid of," I replied, "I'll never forget how his head hit the low diving board, blood gushing into the deep end. Miss Decker ran to slide open the glass doors for an ambulance. She was hysterical."

"I'm gonna screw up in front of the boys. I just know it." Judy whined. "It's so humiliating."

I squinted at the wall clock. Without my glasses, I could barely make out its black hands. "There's not much time left of class," I whispered. "Coach won't get to us today."

Judy nodded.

Lines to the diving board were shortening. I slipped back in the pool and practiced my crawl to correct my breathing technique.

"Karen, it's your turn!"

At that instant, the bell rang. Wet bodies scrambled out of the pool.

"I'll try it next time," I shouted back, "Have to get to French class."

"Now!" The teacher stood with arms akimbo, "You stalled long enough."

Zipping by me, Judy whispered, "Good luck." Pulling off her bathing cap, she began towel-drying her hair.

Slowly climbing out of the pool, I headed for the low board where Miss Decker was perched. She delivered the same rote instructions—your back to the pool, feet halfway on the board, spring with arms in the air, arch back, bend knees to the chest, transfer weight to the front of your body.

I was cornered. I had no choice. "I hate you," I wanted to scream.

Do it – get it over with.

It was hard to concentrate on a skill that my body simply could not do. My thoughts focused on the little time I would have left in the locker room.

Skip drying chlorine-infused hair. Slip pantyhose on wet legs, careful not to tear them. Race to class without getting caught running in the halls.

Facing my tormentor, I sprang backwards. My body landed hard on the water's surface in a stinging backward belly flop. I knew I forgot to arch my back.

Plunging into eight-foot water depth, I panicked in weight-lessness and disorientation.

Which way is up? Don't struggle. No fear. My mother almost drowned when she was a girl. I refused to inherit her fear of swimming.

Calming myself, I slowly allowed my body to surface. Alone in the pool, I treaded water while circling to locate Coach. Still on the diving board with arms folded and eyes squinting, her pock-marked face smirked.

I wanted to yell, "Yup, you'll always be the better swimmer."

Mercifully, no one was there to witness my pitiful attempt. I wiped the water streaming down my face and swam to the stairs. Heading to the locker room, I did not turn around. My back stung, but I refused to break down.

Show no tears.

Sitting in French class, my dripping hair soaked through my flowered dress. I felt all eyes on me but did not dare look around. I tried to concentrate on translating passages from *The Count of the Monte Cristo.*

Growing up at a time when students did not whine to their parents, I "bucked up" and endured bullies like Miss Decker. Unseen scars are the hardest to heal, scars that have tarnished my sense of community with the school despite my academic success. Feeling quite alone, I withdrew from my classmates. What I felt was low self-worth. Why did it take so little for an insignificant teacher in an insignificant class to demean a struggling student?

My anger diminished as decades flew by. As an educator, I discovered that young people who scored on the lower end of the bell curve possessed other skills. They were all intelligent, despite setbacks to learning. Fear of being humiliated forced them to avoid class participation or oral reading. Many developed bad attitudes. Some considered school as a prison sentence to endure until they reached the age of sixteen to legally drop out. For challenged students, I learned to use compassion, not mistreatment.

One year, my school instituted a tracking system. This meant that students were divided into high-, medium-, and low-skilled classes. The latter group knew that they were thrown in together as the "dumb" class. Teachers tended to "water-down" the curriculum for them. I soon realized that they could understand important concepts and abstract ideas as capably as the higher-level students. It took much encouragement.

To reward my low group for performing well on a history unit, I promised to take them fishing. They were rural kids who loved to hunt, farm, and fish.

On a sunny and warm May afternoon, we hopped on a bus to a nearby fishing pond. I announced prizes for the longest, the largest, and the most fish. Students proudly carried their treasured equipment—fishing poles, tackle boxes, nets—to a prime fishing spot.

A warm breeze blew through the weeping willows surrounding the pond. Everyone seemed engaged and comfortable in an environment they preferred over a classroom. Quiet conversations broke the silence.

I should have been content to circulate around to my fisherman to share their enjoyment. Instead, I tried my hand at fishing. Witnessing my husband bait a hook many times, I thought it would be easy.

It did not take students long to realize how awkward and unskilled I was at baiting a hook or casting a line. To begin with, I did not like touching worms, so they took turns piercing the slimy creatures on my barbed hook.

"All ya gotta do is spear the hook through the worm, like this, then slide it toward the top," Luke, with dyslexia, explained. "Don't worry, worms can't feel pain. Make sure you pierce the worm in another spot to secure it on the hook. You don't want it to wiggle away."

I could hardly look at the pink s-shape impaled on its hook, thrashing and squirming for dear life. I was thankful that students took care of that task.

Spontaneous laughter erupted after my casted line landed in a tree branch. Volunteers ran to unravel the line from the willow leaves and gently encouraged me to start again.

Josh, who hates school, laid down his pole and stepped up to demonstrate how to cast.

"Just flick your wrist to the side," he explained, then gently tossed the line into the pond. The hook made a tiny splash and slowly sank.

"Wow, very smooth," I said, "Let me try."

Josh showed a competent side that I have never seen in my classroom. Surrounded by academics, it must have been hard for him to fit in. School was clearly out of his element. I knew what that felt like.

I succeeded in casting after two attempts. Everyone applauded. With thirty minutes left, they each took turns taking care of me. This allowed time for their own serious fishing.

"I got her," Grant, my history buff, yelled when it was his turn.

The next day, students entered my classroom with excitement, eager to brag about prizes they won and the expertise they lent to the teacher.

"Let's go fishing again," shouted Clara, who is test-anxious, "That was a blast."

"With your talents, maybe we will," I said. "I am grateful that you all helped me. If there was a prize for the most dreadful fishing, I'd award it to myself."

"You were really struggling," said Mia, who reads below grade level, "But with some practice, you'll get the hang of it."

Heads nodded with shouts of "yeah."

I smiled and said, "My tangled lines created a frustrating problem. You all showed patience that I did not have. Thanks for stepping up. I learned so much."

Faces were beaming.

"By the way, did any of you see a similarity between my struggles learning how to fish and your struggles learning history?"

Voices gushed around the classroom:

"We struggle in school like you struggled yesterday. But you kept at it and became a fisherman."

"I guess we should keep trying at school. Sometimes, I just don't want to. It's so hard."

"Some people are better than others at things, but that shouldn't stop us from trying."

"We shouldn't put down the ones who need help."

"Mrs. Hempson wasn't ashamed to accept help, and we shouldn't either."

"We stopped laughing once we figured out what you were doing wrong. We know what it feels like to be laughed at."

Standing in front of my maturing adolescents, I swelled with pride. They understood what some adults did not learn—compassion.

17

LIFE IS GOLDEN

TRACY CHAMBERLAIN HIGGINBOTHAM

It is 5 a.m. on a typical school day. I rise from bed to do my daily yoga regimen. The house is enveloped in darkness until I turn on my television to hear my instructor tell me in her calming voice to open up my heart to the energy of the morning. I feel my soul breathe in the peacefulness of a new day. As I finish the invigorating workout the room begins to brighten with a glow of early light. A new day has started and I feel blessed.

As I walk up the stairs to my sons' room, I feel the same rush of emotion I did when I checked on them as babies sleeping in their cribs. Except now my oldest son's six-foot three-inch body dangles off this bed and my youngest son's mop of long brown hair hides his face. As I gently kiss them good morning, they roll over and sigh contently knowing they have a few more minutes of peace before their school day begins. As I open up their window blinds, their room becomes illuminated with a glow that warms and energizes my soul.

The morning soon becomes chaotic as these big lumbering bodies rush around the house trying to make the school bus stop on time. As they run out the door, the soft colors of early morning are gone and replaced by the clear light of day. They are off to school and I settle down at my home office to run my business.

Gracing my desk are three sentimental objects—an American Eagle award given to me as a United States Small Business Administration Women in Business Champion, a photograph of me holding a lacrosse stick with my oldest son and his teenage lacrosse friends, and a photograph of me with my two sons. All three items remind me every day how powerful my choice was to become both a stay-at-home mother and a woman entrepreneur.

They say women are more likely to become entrepreneurs if they have female role models. I fit that statistic perfectly. My mother owned a clothing boutique as well as a ski shop with my father. My aunt owned restaurants and a real estate company. I remember how happy they were running their businesses while finding time to spend with their families. In the late 1960s, they were pioneering women balancing work and family for the first time in generations. Their independence and zest for a more modern life than women before them must have sparked an entrepreneurial spirit in my soul that lay dormant until I became a mother.

Both my mother and aunt had the built-in convenience of my grandmother who babysat her six grandchildren when her daughters needed to work. My grandfather was the cook of their Italian household making delicious traditional meals with fresh ingredients from his one-acre garden, and sweet treats like Pizza Fritte, which was fried dough dripping in melted butter and rolled in sugar. Every meal was complete with fresh orange juice or fresh cow's milk.

One early morning in my household, I started to awaken my sons with my morning kiss, when something deep inside of me awakened too. I realized I didn't want to rush my sons out of bed anymore to bring them to a daycare center just to hurry to my events management job, and wish my day away because I wanted to be with them. I also knew I loved my profession. At that moment, I flashed back to my mother and aunt working in their businesses and my grandparent's care of us. In that golden glow of morning, the dormant entrepreneurial spirit awoke in me. I looked at the rising sun and knew I was going to start my own event management company out of my home where I could be a more present mother in my sons' lives. It was the dawning of a new day in my career and my life.

Starting a business can be exhilarating and terrifying at the same time. I knew I could count on my decade of event planning experience, education, female role models, and passion for my profession to provide a solid foundation to launch my company. My first clients were individuals who worked with me before and trusted my abilities. Their confidence combined with a strong purpose and determination gave me all I needed to begin. I knew I couldn't let this golden opportunity pass me by. I knew I could create the life I desired in these modern times.

Shortly after becoming a home-based female entrepreneur, I realized I needed to surround myself with other women who were taking the same risks. I discovered an organization of women, who met monthly to discuss the pros and cons of being business owners. Open communication, exchange of ideas, and unshakable support from these women ignited my early business success. One year later I developed a deep passion for aiding and inspiring other women entrepreneurs and became the organization's leader which surprisingly became a nine-year assignment as female entrepreneurship grew as a career in our region.

One of my favorite members in the group was a boisterous, older female who once said, "To be a smart woman entrepreneur, you must set a course for your business, but if the road starts to naturally bend in another direction, you must follow the curve and see where it leads you." After ten years of running my first company and nine years as the leader of the growing organization for women business owners, I remembered her words and created my second company dedicated to promoting women entrepreneurship all over New York State. I launched the news at a gathering of 500 women at an event that celebrates and applauds women for taking chances. This was my chance, my chance to help even more women make the same choice I made looking out my sons' window one golden morning.

The eagle statue on my desk reminded me every day that I worked on behalf of women entrepreneurs everywhere helping them to move towards their own bright entrepreneurial future. It also represented a strong belief by the business community that I had made a positive impact on women entrepreneurship. In a file drawer were copies of newspaper columns called "Ask the Entrepreneur" for our community's newspaper which allowed me to share my business acumen with both men and women on a bi-weekly basis for eleven years.

The second item is a photograph of me holding a lacrosse stick with my sixteen-year-old son and his lacrosse friends taken after they challenged me to a lacrosse contest with their junior varsity goalie. I was wearing my favorite pink shirt that stated, "Well behaved women rarely make history." The photo is a token of the challenge I took on with these young men, hoping they would see that girls and women can do anything boys and men can do. I wore it proudly even though I lost the contest but won their respect. Later my son said, "Having a feminist mother means you think women rule the world, but today we proved you otherwise." I answered him, "I went easy on your friend, you know!"

The photograph of my two sons reminds me that I will never regret the personal and professional decisions I have made to be the best mother I can be while being the best woman I can be. When my life is over, I hope a sun is rising on the eastern horizon, more women are achieving business success because of my dedication to them and their companies, and my two wonderful sons appreciate the power of women to make the right choices for their lives, careers, and home life. Important choices create a ripple effect that changes the world.

As another day ends and the glow of the setting sun now shines on my desk, I look out the window and feel peaceful knowing tomorrow brings another golden opportunity for me to awaken to a glorious new day and to shine more rays of inspiration and hope to women entrepreneurs everywhere. Life is golden.

Another day has ended and I feel blessed.

18

SAVING HER

AMY JAMES

We arrived in Cleveland at 2 a.m. in a snowstorm. Exiting the interstate and winding our way through the peaceful, snowy roads of a city park, we emerged into the labyrinth of medical buildings that constituted the clinic. I felt like a stranger, separated from everything that had ever been familiar. My mother was in the dark sky somewhere, hooked up to a ventilator in a small plane, existing in some netherworld that protected her—I hoped—from the fear I was sure she would have felt. She did not like to fly. My sister was with her. My sister-in-law and I waited in the hotel adjacent to the clinic for news that the plane had landed. My brother stayed behind with our father, six hours east in upstate New York where our drive had begun. The storm continued. Our phone did not ring. By the time my sister finally walked in the hotel room door at 4 a.m., I had convinced myself, quietly, that my mother had died en route. The necessity of quickly replacing not the expected one, but two heart valves in our small, local hospital was too much for her; we had gone to an extreme, and her body, in its weakened state, had not been able to cope. In our fervent hope for her survival, we had killed her. But the news from my sister was simply that the normally one-hour drive to the airport from our local hospital had turned into two and a half hours in a cramped ambulance, and then the storm had been too fierce for the plane to take off for some time. After that, there was the check-in at the clinic and the consultations with the sizable medical team that had been waiting for the plane to arrive. We slept groggily for a few hours.

At 7 a.m. our phone rang and we were asked to meet our mother's surgeon at 7:30. We arrived at the clinic and were greeted at the elevator by a very professional male nurse, then escorted to meet Dr. Petterson. We had heard him referred to as "the Wizard," a man able to fix anything. We had reached the Emerald City of hospitals, where we could find Starbucks and sushi in the cafeteria, internet-ready computers in every waiting room, and from many rooms and corridors, cold, sweeping views of Lake Erie.

The three of us held hands as we waited for this tall, angular Swedish stranger to tell us whether he thought he could fix what had gone wrong with the heart surgery my mother had had two weeks earlier. Although he had never spoken with her, he told me he had heard from her local doctors that she was a very spunky lady; a fighter. And so it was that three hours later she was wheeled into the operating room by a team of doctors larger than any I had seen on a television medical drama. We smoothed her hair, rubbed her feet, sang to her and—seeing that she was mostly conscious and aware—tried to keep her informed. Still intubated, she could only look at us with wide eyes and nod in wonder when we asked her, "Do you know where you are?" "You understand you're at the Cleveland Clinic, right?" "Do you remember the plane ride?" When I asked her what song she wanted me to sing, she (a master at charades and still possessing good arm mobility) indicated that she wanted to hear, "Somewhere over the Rainbow." Her name, incidentally, was

Dorothy. A few minutes after I finished singing, the Wizard came to take her.

The next six months have become a series of impressions, stories, and conversations that I am always hoping will fall into a neat narrative that will explain everything: the ensuing, and surprising, series of clear, dry six-hour drives from my hometown to Cleveland and back; the beautiful family from Indiana that I met in the waiting room who watched over my kids as I hovered for hours in the ICU; the smell of the coconut foot cream we bought to remind my mother of summer; the bossy Russian nurse, Tatiana, who scolded my mother but somehow made us all love her because she tried so hard; the sound of my cell phone ring that I grew to dread; the letters I faxed her every day when I could not be there to give her the will I feared she might be losing; leaving my children and returning to them again; leaving her and returning to her again; and above everything, strangely, the seemingly almost constant clear, blue winter sky of Cleveland.

The world springs to life again even when someone is dying. February turned to late March and my mother, still on the ventilator but now with a tracheotomy, sang "Happy Birthday" to my brother on the phone by "plugging" the trach with a special device that allowed her to speak. That was a Sunday. We sat up together, reading the New York Times and watching a boat on the lake from her window on the tenth floor. She wrote me long notes, as it was too tiring for her to speak more than a minute or two at a time. That day the note said that she looked forward to helping someone else make it through this experience. I returned to my own family late that afternoon, this time feeling buoyant. The sun was brilliant as I neared Buffalo, coming up over the crest of a small rise to see the eastern tip of Lake Erie shimmering before me. There was still bright snow on the ground surrounding the lake; Carole King was singing "Only Love is Real." In that instant, all was right with the world.

When someone we love is just a few precarious inches away from death's grasp, we have to take these moments and live in them.

A week later, my mother was back in intensive care with an infection. And so it went: a few days of relative improvement, of breathing on her own, of actually being able to speak on the telephone with my father, who—unable to travel—had not seen her since the beginning of February, of writing long notes and smiling and "chatting" (in her own way) to the doctors and nurses. Then would come the beginning of a fever, a consultation with confused groups of doctors who could never find the source of the infection, and then several more days in the ICU where she could not sit up or eat solids or have visitors more than a few hours a day.

In this day and age, death seems unthinkable to us when we have medically-equipped airplanes, comfortable cars that can get us anywhere we want to go, artificial hearts, state-of-the-art dialysis equipment, and hospital cafeterias full of attractive teams of brilliant doctors eating egg-white omelets and made-to-order protein smoothies. But death is something else entirely. Dying takes on a life of its own apart from doing. It is about being and not being. And in what seems like the blink of an eye, no matter how long someone has been suffering, we have to be able to say, "Okay, it is done." But the problem was that my mother simply did not seem like the kind of person who would die, and never in all that time expressed a wish to do so.

We needed my parents to see each other. They had been married for 55 years. My mother seemed to be ever so slightly losing touch. My father had caregivers during the day and either my brother or me with him in the early evenings, but sat alone at night with the dog, smoking cigars and watching the Yankees or Turner Classic Movies and waiting for my mother to come home. Raised in wealth with remote parents and a much younger brother, he had never gotten the hang of socializing. At the Naval Academy and later in service as a gunnery officer on a destroyer in Korea, he'd taken on his duties quietly but not without qualm (as a teenager, he'd wanted to be a poet—an officer of words, not artillery). And despite the bustling household of my childhood—with three children, two dogs, one cat, and nearly every kid from up the street running in and out—he still depended on my mother to be his link to the living world. He had always preferred a quiet day or evening with her to anything else, and her absence magnified the fact that, for the most part, he did not know what to say or do with any of us as we circled around him during these last months.

Somewhat triumphantly but nervously, we moved my mother to a hospital closer to home—only three hours away—that could support her need for both dialysis and ventilator weaning. We rarely acknowledged death, but instead focused on the possible. My parents raised us with a work ethic and we felt that if we just kept on we could work our way out of death just as my mother had worked her way out of the poverty in which she began. I drove my father down to see her at the end of April. The reunion was nothing like I or any of the nurses expected. She, the talker, could not talk. He, the reserved, did not talk. Mostly, he read the paper while she stared at the wall. I left them alone for a couple of hours, but when I returned it was clear to me that they had been unable to communicate. In this manner, we spent a full day and the next morning. On the way home, my father and I crossed swords, quietly, over whether or not he could smoke a cigar in the car. In the end, he accommodated my request not to do so, but now I wonder why I cared.

She began to go into what the new doctors called "fugue states," which meant that she was entirely unresponsive. During the first of these, I raced to the hospital and slipped into her room. Her transistor radio was on and Louis Armstrong was singing, "Love, to me, is like a summer day. When it's gone, the memory will stay. Still and warm and peaceful. Now the days are getting long, I can sing my summer song." I had heard Dave Brubeck's "Summer Song" a hundred times, but never knew it had words until this late May day in my mother's room at Wilkes-Barre General Hospital, where her own mother had had a successful heart surgery in 1966. She lay still as a stone. The sun beat down on the window blinds that she now insisted always be closed. I parted them and watched the world go on below me—the lone kid riding a bike past the nearly identical rows of ragtag old mill houses, the flowers blooming next to the decaying sidewalks. Just over the horizon was the town of Plymouth, where my mother had been an underfed fourth child in a family of seven living on "Welsh Hill," a street built on the coal mines where all the back yards ran together. For sport, they would let go of her brother's baby carriage at the top of the hill and watch it fly toward Shawnee Ave into the arms of the oldest sibling, Betty. In the evenings they'd sing along with her father's ukulele in their living room with the scratchy turquoise furniture. That night I dreamt she smiled at me. The next morning, when I walked into her room, she did. I canceled the call to the hospice my siblings and I had planned, and we were all back to saving her again.

My mother died on the 24th of June, with four of us at her side—her brood, her steady sidekicks through life, and now death. My father died on the 13th of November with three of us there, navigating as best we could to an unknown destination. I held their hands as each took their last breaths. It is something to watch how easily and quickly that happens. One minute, the chest is rising and falling, the next minute it is not. You go get a nurse and say, "She's gone," or "He's gone." The nurse comes in, looks at her watch, and then says, "Stay as long as you want." You sit around the hospital bed crying or laughing weakly or feeling relieved or feeling bereft, feeling grateful for parents and siblings, feeling that there is nothing at all left to say. Later on, you might wonder if you could have done something differently, if you could have changed the outcome. But when someone first dies you give over to the force of the universe and for a few minutes it even seems beautiful, as beautiful and miraculous as a birth.

19

PLANT SWAP

SARAH L. MAWHORTER

Cornflower and Queen Anne's lace dance on the narrow shoulder of Old Seneca Turnpike between Syracuse and Skaneateles, New York. Last July, Matt and I drove this way from Syracuse for the first time, jittery with the hope that the Skaneateles rental house might work out. That first summer of the pandemic, we felt the urge to get out of our downtown apartment with its shared hallways, elevators, and stuffy air to a place where we could open our front door and walk outside.

Our one-year lease on the Skaneateles house is up this week. Now we're moving again, this time leaving Central New York entirely to set out for the Netherlands. We've driven back and forth between Skaneateles and Syracuse, dispatching dry goods and furniture to friends, eating farewell meals on porches, donating books to the library, squeezing in appointments with our beloved optometrist and less-beloved dentist—for who knows what Dutch vision and dental care will be like? We're paring down accumulated detritus, provisioning for an intercontinental move, and putting miles on the car we are about to sell. Saying goodbye.

On this trip toward Syracuse, I'm driving solo. The back seats of our Subaru hatchback are folded down for hauling. The trunk holds our last remaining houseplants. Taking the freeway would be a few minutes faster; the country turnpike gives me time to settle my mind. I lean into each rise, bend, and dip of the road across the glacier-softened landscape. I roll down the windows. The scent of summer fields fills the car.

***

The jade plant in the trunk began as a cutting from one of the mammoth jades growing next to my grandmother's driveway in Goleta, California—years ago, back when I lived just a few hours' drive from her house. Once as I was leaving after a weekend visit, Gran broke off a flowering stem and handed it to me through my open car window. "These jades all come from a cutting your grandfather's mother gave to me from her garden when we were newlyweds. She was such a kind mother-in-law."

I didn't know what to do with this rootless branch, so I left it on the kitchen windowsill. At some point, the flowers fell off and the stem shriveled. I'd killed Gran's jade! I panicked and stuck it in a pot outside, where I didn't have to watch it die. When I remembered to check on it a few months later, it seemed miraculously plump after the winter rains. Back inside, I gave it the sunniest spot in our apartment and marveled at each new oval leaf it produced.

***

Four years ago, just married, Matt and I drove nearly 3,000 miles east from California to Syracuse. Matt had landed a tenure-track professorship at Syracuse University. There were no apparent jobs for me in Syracuse, but I could finish the second year of my Berkeley postdoc working remotely. We brought along the New Zealand fern from our first apartment together, a mini agave my mom gave me for my office and Gran's jade.

Matt was skeptical that the plants could survive the 10-day road trip at the height of summer, but I saw no reason to leave them behind. With heavy lobbying on my part, he conceded that we would give it a try. Packing the car to the limit, I contrived gaps between suitcases for the plants. Whenever we stopped along the way, I took the plants out and set them in the shade so they wouldn't cook.

In downtown Syracuse, the jade and agave adapted to the windowsill of our apartment overlooking Salina Street. We lived a block south of where the long-abandoned Erie Canal once gave logic to the grand stone and brick buildings along its banks. Five floors up, the plants witnessed pelting rain and blizzards entirely foreign to the Southern California gardens of my foremothers. Forced air heating provided the dry warmth succulents love. The fern, too, seemed happy enough in the corner by Matt's record player.

The move was harder on me. Recognizing that I was in a tough position as Matt's "trailing spouse" working remotely, his department chair finagled me an office in an SU research center and an invitation to attend their seminars. Over the first lunch buffet, I introduced myself to the white-haired center director, hoping to connect over our shared interest in demography.

"Ah, Sarah!" he replied genially, "You're Matt Young's wife?"

I nodded.

"You're a problem for us," he continued in the same friendly tone, "We thought about whether we should offer you a job too, but we decided we didn't need to."

I couldn't think of a response, so I smiled as brightly as I could and concentrated on the tray of turkey sandwiches. I mostly stayed home after that, working deadline to deadline, keeping my toes on the second-lowest rung on the academic ladder.

***

I missed walking. Over the years together in Los Angeles, Matt and I rambled in all directions. In the evenings after dinner, we walked up and down our local hills in Los Feliz, or headed south towards Silverlake, or maybe east into Atwater Village. Sometimes we'd drive to meet friends or try a restaurant in Culver City, Little Tokyo, Venice, Miracle Mile, Echo Park, then start our walk from there. We often kept going well into night, as coyotes yipped and howled in the foothills. More than once we startled a skunk on its midnight rounds. Even on familiar ground, we discovered new permutations, hidden staircases, gardens, and views. In the mornings we climbed Mount Hollywood in Griffith Park. We joined a cast of regulars to watch the sunrise over the Los Angeles basin, fully gridded with boulevards and avenues stretching to the ports of Los Angeles and Long Beach and the gleaming Pacific Ocean beyond.

Starting in downtown Syracuse, we had two viable walking routes: the Creekwalk heading north to Onondaga Lake, or east towards the SU campus and Westcott. Both routes took us under freeways, across uninviting expanses of vacant buildings and concrete parking lots between the more scenic stretches. It wasn't such a good idea to walk the streets at night, even together. As winter set in, it became clear that the expensive jacket I'd bought in October wasn't going to keep me warm. I needed a real coat, yet I stubbornly made do with layering: another good reason to stay indoors.

My days were unstructured.

***

One Thursday afternoon in mid-January, Matt was off teaching. I remembered seeing a poster about writing classes at the YMCA, just a few blocks away. I looked it up. It was already past the signup deadline for the winter classes, but there was a number to call.

One ring, and then a cheerful voice: "Hello, you're speaking with Georgia at the Downtown Writers Center."

I took a breath, "I recently moved to Syracuse, and I'm interested in taking writing classes. I realize it might be too late to sign up—are there any spots left?"

"Let's see, which classes? There may still be space."

By the end of the call, I was enrolled in an intro course on micro-memoir and a workshop called the "Winter Flow" led by Georgia herself.

The next Thursday at 1:25 p.m. I walked two blocks to the YMCA's back entrance through late January slush. In the low-ceilinged bowels of the YMCA, seven of us came to sit around a conference table just a little too large for the windowless room. Georgia sat by the open door with a whiteboard behind her, auburn curls gleaming under fluorescent light. She paused for us to remove our coats and settle, closed the door, and invited us to introduce ourselves. Denny, Carol, Jackie, Gwenlyn, Kathy... everyone else drove to come downtown, from Westcott, Fayetteville, Baldwinsville, and even Ithaca. Most were retired, with time to write and meet midday; I was the youngest in the room by a few decades.

Georgia explained how we would exchange our writing via email on Mondays and come prepared to discuss each piece during our two-hour workshops on Thursdays, giving our written comments at the end of class. Each of us would submit three pieces over the eight-week session.

"Pay attention: you can learn just as much from reading others' writing as from critiques of your own work."

Soon I received the first batch of writing in my inbox. I read Carol's stories of a tough childhood knocking between Syracuse and Jamesville, leavened with glimmers of humor and understanding.

Kathy's stories of her childhood neighbors Frank and Bertha, her uncle's Italian deli. Gwenlyn's experiences of friendship, violence, and healing. Jackie's escapades parenting her two irrepressible sons. Denny's Irish grandmother's double life.

I was hooked on their stories.

For my part, I shared stories about cycling down Santa Monica Boulevard with my Uncle James, how Gran learned to fly her little Cessna airplane, and the moment over tacos de pescado when I first felt the full force of Matt's abiding love.

One Thursday we were getting ready to leave class, trading our printed comments across the table. I had workshopped a tough story about my Uncle James' recent death. Carol beckoned me over and handed me her critique, saying something under her breath.

"Can you repeat that?" I asked. "I couldn't quite hear you."

"May I give you a hug?"

"Of course." I reached out to her.

Carol held back for a moment and directed, "Now, while we hug, we're going to close our eyes and take three breaths in and out together."

Carol was surprisingly strong for someone in her eighties. In her arms, my loneliness receded.

Something else happened in that workshop: Syracuse became more than the site of my exile from California. Borrowing memories, I started to see the streets and buildings as the settings for my new friends' lives—maybe someday a place for my own stories.

***

Now we're moving away. Matt's job at SU went sideways, and after a mad scramble of academic job applications, we find ourselves moving to Leiden, in South Holland. This time we will both begin new jobs as assistant professors. A few precious books, kitchen implements, and our office chairs are already on a cargo ship across the Atlantic. The rest of our belongings are headed to Worchester, Massachusetts, for indefinite storage in my brother's basement.

This time, the plants are staying behind. I had an inkling that plants weren't allowed into Europe. A few weeks back I tracked down the number for the regional USDA horticultural inspector, who kindly explained that any plants would need to spend at least six months in a commercial export nursery with multiple inspections before possible transfer to Europe. Even more wildly impractical than driving plants across a continent.

If I can't bring the plants with me, I'll give them good homes. So I'm on my way to Carol's house for a goodbye potluck dinner, with my contribution of houseplants: the three we'd brought from California, joined by another dozen or so acquired during our four years in Central New York.

Carol greets me at her door; the others are out back. A small gathering, as we still need to be cautious about COVID. I put down my armful of plants and walk to the sunny deck, where Georgia, Gwenlyn, Kathy, and Jackie are already sitting. Wait, Jackie?! She sold her house and moved to South Carolina months ago. Gleeful, Georgia explains, "Jackie said she'd be back in town for the weekend, and I asked if she could stay one extra day to be here with us."

Carol has orchestrated quite a spread for us, starring rotisserie chicken and Syracuse salt potatoes, Kathy's broccoli-cauliflower salad, and Gwenlyn's quinoa, rice, and farro, finishing up with strawberries and whipped cream. We eat and talk and laugh until the sunlight softens. It's time to go.

The activity of giving away the houseplants makes our goodbyes a little easier to bear. Carol doesn't want a houseplant, especially one so freighted with nostalgia. "I'll just kill it." Jackie can't bring one home on the plane. Kathy accepts the fern, Gwenlyn a lithops, and Georgia takes the agave and jade.

One last three-breath hug, and I start back for Skaneateles. Halfway home, I slow as the road sinks towards the Town of Marcellus. I scan the signs on the left of the road and pull over just before the road veers off for Skaneateles. There it is, the sign I saw this morning: PLANT SWAP / Need a plant / Take a plant / Share your surplus. I remove the remaining plants from the trunk and place them carefully on the shelves, positioned for visibility from the road. I drive off for home in an empty car.

20

BREAKING AWAY

MARISSA MONTGOMERY

As soon as I awoke, I knew the dream was a turning point.

Running through the streets of my neighborhood, Bill, my estranged husband, chased me. In a stern, manipulative voice, he used his usual methods to reel me in.

"Cut this out. Come back now. You know you're overreacting."

I felt the old weakness, the temptation to give in, but this time, I kept going. Coming round a corner, I spotted my house, the house I had recently purchased. It was a large Victorian with a wrap-around porch, painted white and brown, it resembled the house my grandparents owned when I was a child. I quickly climbed the porch steps but did not go inside. Having cleared the corner, Bill approached, but before he could ascend the stoop, I turned around to face him. Holding up my left hand, I signaled him to stop. Then, with my fist clenched, I lifted my right elbow horizontally at my side, as a large owl landed on my arm.

"Stop," I said. "It's no use. This is my home."

Lingering with the images, as I recorded the dream, I was certain it confirmed what I had previously intuited.

I called my sister. Of all people, I had to share this with her.

"Lizzie, we can change the way we experience the past."

***

In my first month of college, I met Denny at a dorm mixer. A funny tangle of coincidences brought us together. For the first half-hour, the Robert Hall rec room remained segregated as if an invisible line divided it down the center. The guys from first-north, the "all-male" floor, crowded around the pool table as they cast covert glances at third-east's residents, "all female." With their big eighties' hair, they lined the wall on the far side of the ping-pong table, watching their floor mates laugh with coy embarrassment as they missed one volley after another. Players and spectators, first-north and third-east, were all clearly distracted by the occupants on the opposite side of the room.

Thinking I was above it all, I hiked myself up onto a four-foot-high counter. Astrid, my art student roommate, quickly joined me. Having the best seats in the house, we surveyed the room for cute guys. Like a magnet, my gaze landed on Denny. He was hard to miss. Tall and blond, he had a commanding presence. Leaning over the pool table in a t-shirt and jeans that barely hid his muscle tone, he lined up his shot, then pocketed the eight ball with a forceful, but agile grace. As his next opponents prepared the table for a new game, Denny set aside the pool stick with an air of triumph then sauntered by me on his way to the beer keg. I made use of the opportunity.

"You look like Mike."

He stopped short of his destination and turned to me, mildly perplexed.

"You know, in the film, Breaking Away."

Watching his smile stretch ear to ear, I knew I had hit my mark.

Laughing, he sprang cougar-like to take a seat on the counter next to me. Using his fingers he combed his broad, blond bangs away from his eyes, then extended his hand, "Denny."

"What about your game?"

Signaling he was done, he turned to me and began speaking in the affable manner I would soon adore. Within minutes, the room and the people around us faded away, as our conversation turned over one surreal leaf and then another.

For starters, Denny not only looked like Dennis Quaid in Breaking Away, he shared his name, and being a triathlete, he told me he loved that movie.

"It taught me to push myself past my limits, to reach for my best."

"I know what you mean. I'm not a cyclist or a swimmer, but I am a distance runner—to win, you have to persevere and in the final stretch, you need to reach deep for that extra kick."

Denny nodded his head in full agreement, as I continued. "I started running meets in elementary school. I was small, so my coach assumed I was a sprinter, but it turned out, I was better at distance."

In my mind, I replayed the last lap of the 3200 meters, when you finally catch sight of the finish line. The coach said I was lucky. I could always find that extra reserve of energy that would launch me into overdrive. Pain and exhaustion would evaporate as my limbs carried me forward on a cresting wave of euphoria.

"There's nothing like a runner's high. Have you experienced that?"

"Oh yeah," he chuckled, once again flipping his bangs aside. I took note of the freckles on his neck, "It's better than an upper!"

Letting that reference to pharmaceuticals go by, I asked, "Where are you from?" We soon discovered we not only attended the same junior high, we also belonged to the same track team, but strangely had no memory of each other.

My jaw dropped. "I can't believe it! How's that possible?"

"I was quiet back then—a late bloomer. Believe it or not, before my growing spurt, I was short for my age."

Used to being the smallest in class, I could relate.

The next day in the dining hall, a tray clasped in his hand, Denny strode up to the table my floormates and I had adopted as "our spot."

"You want to join us tonight? We're going to the Matador—it's two-for-one tequila shots."

Denny and his first-north coterie of friends had lost no time mapping out a weekly schedule of drink specials at the local bars.

"I don't have an ID." I was seventeen.

"Don't worry, we'll find a way to sneak you in."

It was Sunday night. Astride and I had planned to spend the rest of the evening in the library, but overcome by his Dennis Quaid smile, I nodded.

"I'm in."

Under the table, Astrid covertly pinched my leg. Figuring she was jealous, I swept her hand away.

Monday morning, for the first time, I missed my music theory class. It wasn't the last. For three successive weeks, each night we trekked to a different bar. Denny and Mitchell, the music major who lived at the end of Denny's floor, were determined to see how long they could carry the streak. My grades started slipping. I knew it but didn't care. When the Robert Hall Halloween costume party rolled around, we appeared together in our costumes—Denny was Julius Caesar, and I, his glamorous, but somewhat garishly bedecked consort. We were the royal couple at the center of our half-stoned, drunken party crowd. In truth, Denny was our Prince Hal. A golden boy, he'd always planned to go pre-law, but a DWI in high school and subsequent probation for drug possession had ruined his chances at Ivy League. Denny's record didn't phase me. Perhaps it felt oddly familiar. I was a baby in the crib when my father's brazen antics required my grandmother to call in a favor from the governor. Denny's father was a high-powered, real-estate lawyer, who'd pulled strings to get Denny a lighter sentence. That's all I ever knew about the nuclear family Denny never introduced me to.

That first semester felt like a beatnik adventure. Out from under my parent's strict control, Denny was my road to freedom. He taught me to play billiards. He also slipped me my first dose of LSD. "Stick out your tongue." No warning. "Just swallow it. Trust me."

We blew off school to follow concert tours—the Rolling Stones, Frank Zappa, and the Grateful Dead. Then oddly, when winter break came around, I hardly heard from Denny. He was busy re-uniting with high school friends, while I worked overtime to save enough money for the spring semester. When the time approached to return to school, Denny finally phoned me.

"I may have to take time off from school."

My heart sank like a rock. After one semester of non-stop partying, Denny had burned through his college savings. When his parents discovered he was on academic probation, they refused to finance his habits. Denny was broke. He had no cash to buy textbooks, much less go to the bars.

I responded without thinking. "Don't worry Denny, I'll pay for you."

We devised a strategy. If Denny and I took the same classes, we could share the books. We both registered for Introduction to

Political Science and Criminal Justice 101—not my first choices, but Denny still hoped to follow in his father's footsteps. Sitting side by side in class, once again, we were the royal couple, but I soon noticed I was doing most of the work. I shrugged it off.

I fell in love with the Enlightenment thinkers: Locke, Rousseau, Smith, and Hobbes, I enjoyed taking detailed notes on the readings and started speaking up in class. However, as soon as the leftist students invited me to an after-hours discussion, Denny made it clear he didn't approve. Every now and then, when Denny was busy, I'd sneak off to poly-sci club. Slowly but surely, my college experience, at the least the parts I actually absorbed, had reawakened my intellect. In a sense, I was being radicalized. Denny, on the other hand, despite his reckless youth, was destined to return to the upper-crust establishment he hailed from.

I began to outgrow my boyfriend. After a few incidents of his heavy drinking, I saw another side to him—a deep anger and physical forcefulness. Once, in the midst of a first-north floor party, he grabbed me hard and pulled me against his chest. "You better not leave me." The anger in his eyes frightened me. He kissed me so hard, he bruised my lips.

On St. Patrick's Day, I broke up with him. Leaving straight from criminal justice class, we arrived late afternoon at our favorite bar. By evening Denny was sloppy drunk. Wavering over the pool table, he grabbed a girl he barely knew and tried to kiss her. I walked out and he followed me all the way back to the dorm, tripping repeatedly and swearing he was sorry. I refused to change my mind, in large part because he had humiliated me in front of our friends.

For the next few weeks, he wrote letters claiming he was so heartbroken he couldn't eat. Having gotten a taste of freedom I hadn't realized I had lost, I didn't respond. Up to that point, Denny had dominated my college life. Now I discovered the world I'd been missing. I enjoyed staying up late with my poly-sci friends. Instead of partying, we talked about everything from Dostoyevsky, to Marx, to the wacky exploits of G. Gordon Liddy.

April Fool's Day, I attended a keg party in the dorm, where I bumped into Denny and our old crowd clustered in a corner. I had a feeling I'd find them there, but I chose to go anyway. A part of me missed the days holding court with Denny. Thinking it wouldn't hurt to say hello or even socialize a bit, I approached and was immediately welcomed. Mitchell handed me a beer in a plastic cup and started reminiscing about our many adventures. Denny, seated in the center, kept pulling me into his lap. Confused, I didn't fight much, but as soon as Denny went to the bathroom, I decided it was to time to leave and seek out my other friends. As I headed to the door, Denny intercepted me in the lobby. Taking hold of my elbow with his fist, he forcibly changed my course.

"I need to talk to you. Let's go to the rec room."

Denny ushered me down the stairs through the rec room doors, where we came upon a rowdy game of beer-pong.

Still commanding my elbow, Denny pressed past them. "This way."

He led me down the hallway past the laundry rooms and into a storage room full of stacked chairs and tables. He shut the door. I started to feel uneasy.

Standing under the basement window as the moon backlit his face, he interrogated me. "Are you seeing someone else? One of those poly-sci know-it-alls?"

"Not seriously." I grew annoyed. "Anyway, it's none of your business."

Clenching his fists, his muscles tensed, Denny charged at the window and punched out a pane, then pacing backward like a boxer, he lunged at a stack of chairs. Despite his strength, he couldn't push it over. Violently yanking a chair from the top of the stack, he smashed it against the wall. Terrified, my brain flooded with adrenaline, I bolted out of the door, down the corridor, and out the back exit of the dorm into a dark, deserted, moonlit landscape.

Why did I go this way?

I looped around towards the front of the building but was blocked by large stone terraces, six feet tall. Darting to the right I scrambled up the stone steps I knew were there, but couldn't see. Tripping and scraping myself, I climbed up and out of the backyard to the grassy lawn on the side of the dorm.

I ran.

Looking over my shoulder, I caught Denny's white silhouette, as he ascended the terrace with the limberness of a mountain lion. My feet slipped and kicked up mud as I sprinted across the flat, open space that led to the front of the dorm and its brightly lit entrance. I reached deep for my runner's stride—desperate for a burst of hormones to carry me to safety. But Hermes wings could not outrun Denny's rage. Pumping my legs over the soft, spring grass, he quickly closed in on me.

I could not win this race.

At my heels, Denny swiped his arms at me once, twice, again. I veered right to avoid him, but in my panic, I turned away from the dorm, towards the dark expanse of lawn that stretched all the way to the engineering building. Once again, I ran in the wrong direction. With a quick jolt, I felt Denny grab the hood of my sweatshirt. As I struggled to get free, the sweatshirt almost pulled over my head and off me. Denny grabbed my arm and whipped me around swiftly. He easily overpowered me, as he spun me down, around, onto the dark, damp ground.

It was late, but I saw a few stragglers make their way to their dorms. I screamed, "Help! Help me!"

No one stopped. My mind screeched. Why aren't they helping? I screamed again. "Stop, someone please help me!" After a sunny spring day, a number of Robert Hall's windows were still open. "Someone has to hear me!"

Denny placed his hand over my mouth. Holding me down, my back against the earth, he spouted angry words, spewing spit in my face. The moonlight twisted his image into contrasting grimaces, ribbons of red and white stretched taut by one angry word after another. His eyes once blue, were a dark abyss.

Denny clenched his fist and punched me in the head. He kept punching me, then he bit my face, he bit my left cheek, he bit my lips.

I knew this was it. I would die in this soft, muddy place that already smelled like worms.

That revelation hot-wired my brain and kicked it into overdrive. Denny had been spouting something the entire time. I focused on his words.

"You have to listen to me. Why won't you listen to me? We have to stay together. I love you. You're mine, my girlfriend."

In a soft voice, I responded. "Denny, I'm listening. You're right. I shouldn't have broken up with you."

"No, you shouldn't have." He sounded more like a little boy than a full-grown man.

Relaxing his grip on my collar, he spluttered. "You're mine. I need you."

I spoke in soothing tones. "I understand. I want you to tell me everything. Let's go inside. We'll go to my room and talk it over."

He stopped. "Okay."

We both stood up. All the anger had drained from his limbs. I was shivering.

Knowing this peace was tenuous at best, I continued to play-act. As if nothing had happened, I waved him forward. "Come on, it's cold, let's go inside."

We walked across the lawn to the door, but when we got under the light of the entryway, Denny saw my face. In horror, he yanked his long blond bangs backward. "Oh, my god. Oh, my god."

I had my keys out, ready to open the door. When he extended his arm, I thought to punch me, I ducked. Howling, like a wild animal, he smashed the whole length of his arm across the large picture window next to the door. The crash punctured the night, as the glass collapsed in a cascade that covered the entire entryway. I didn't look, fumbling with my keys in blind terror, I unlocked the door as quickly as possible and ran into the foyer. Denny ran back into the night.

For a brief moment, all my synapses flooded with pure elation, but panic quickly returned. Denny might come back. Hide! I ran through the lobby and up the staircase to my room on the third-east. Desperately searching my pockets, I couldn't find my keys. I must have left them at the front door. Barred access to my dorm room, my body slid down the solid, maple door, until I collapsed onto the hallway floor. Curling into a ball, I started crying, and then lost consciousness.

21

Unexpected Cultural Connections

Mary Nowyj

The late 1960s and 1970s heralded the hippie, love bug, and peace culture over parts of the United States. California had hippies traveling north to south touting free love. Woodstock, NY, got a hold of free love as the musical industry crazed the young people into a dancing frenzy in a farmer's field. A lot was happening on many college campuses across the country. This was a time of young cultural rebellion that indicated change had to be taken especially due to the worldview of destruction and war. Many loved ones and friends were affected by the Vietnam ongoing crisis. I sure was searching for answers for peace, too.

Fresh out of high school as a new college student, I wondered about the differences in belief systems and values others tried to educate me about since childhood. The college experience was meant to enhance learning a new worldview I had only questioned earlier in life. After classes, I would meet with friends at a restaurant to discuss various subjects, especially war. That's when I met the man who would become the love of my life.

His name was Stephen. He came over to talk with me even though I was with other friends.

"May I have a few minutes of your time?" he asked.

I responded, "Not now, sir."

After a few minutes of his persistence, I said, "OK." We connected and had quite an interesting conversation about cultural diversity on the campus. He mentioned he was a Ukrainian immigrant, which intrigued me. I've lived in Syracuse my whole life. It's a wonderful city with many cultural heritages, yet, I never heard about Ukrainians. Eventually, we started dating and he shared how his family came to Syracuse, NY.

Stephen talked about his mother, Paraska, later nicknamed Pearl. He spoke emotionally.

"My mom went through a lot in her lifetime. She survived being taken from her home country of Ukraine in 1938 to work in Germany. When she had to leave her home she felt the sky had changed above her."

Pearl ended up in a small village in Hof und Lembach near Ludwigsburg where her new working home was with a nice German family. There she met a Ukrainian man nearby. Wolodymer worked on the railroad system and would occasionally meet her on weekends at community events. They eventually married and produced two young boys by the end of WWII, from 1945 to 1947.

The family lived in a displaced individuals settlement area until they immigrated to America hoping for a better life. Wolodymer had distant cousins who lived in Marcellus, NY. The family needed recommendations from their local church and village officials as part of the application process. They also needed valid health records. This would take a while to acquire.

By 1952, the process was complete and the family boarded a ship to eventually arrive in the harbor of New York City where the grand lady of the waters was there to welcome them to Ellis Island.

Stephen said, "My mom was seasick the whole time. She hardly ever came out of our cabin during the ocean voyage across the Atlantic to the United States."

At Ellis Island, the family went through the process of immigration with documents and pictures supporting their embarkation. There were many others from different countries. Their new life was about to begin in Marcellus, NY, then, finally to Syracuse where the main Ukrainian church and National Home were well-established.

Stephen said, "There, I grew up knowing more about my Ukrainian heritage."

It was important to continue carrying on the language, religion, and traditions that were so familiar to their ethnic identity. The family adapted to their community eventually finding jobs that would support them during the transition into an unfamiliar lifestyle. Learning English was important as they looked forward to buying a house, communicating with neighbors, and learning how to drive.

By the time I met my gentleman's family, I had my own way of viewing the world I grew up in since childhood. Obviously, there were differences. My American heritage was quite different with representation of French, Dutch-German, and Scottish ancestry. Yet, intrigued by the historical elements his family had survived, I continued to learn more and became embraced in many of the cultural aspects of Ukrainian life. And, his family adopted me into the Ukrainian culture.

A few years later, we were married in the Ukrainian church and raised our family in traditions that encouraged a community connection where we embraced a livelihood that suited both of us. Our life was full of experiences that led to becoming involved with the International Center of Syracuse where we hosted families in our home that were visiting from other countries. Sharing the history of my city was rewarding as I brought many visitors to various places around Central, NY.

Our neighborhood included various ethnic groups. One couple we connected with was from Germany. Christiana had come from Munich. Her husband Rienhard was from East Germany. Both had a wonderful history of their country, which they shared with us, thoroughly. We had a long relationship, then both our husbands got sick and died within months of each other leaving us grieving widows. Christiana and I continued to deepen our relationship.

A few years later, Christiana invited me to visit Munich where she still had an apartment. She wanted to introduce me to German life like I introduced her to Syracuse. I ended up traveling there during the fall. Christiana took me to various places in Germany and Austria, including the village where my husband was born. While there, I revisited the history of my late husband's family, which was extraordinary. Oddly, I sensed that I was going to return to Germany at some point again.

Shortly after returning from my visit to Germany, I received a phone call from my friend, Susan, who knew I went to Germany.

"Mary, I read about a contest in Second Journey titled, Transitions in Life with the Korber Foundation in Germany. They are sponsoring an international contest for an idea exchange. Would you be interested in applying? All we have to do is present an idea that would provide something of interest appealing to Korber Foundation."

I responded, "I do have an idea. How about a bereavement garden?"

I had belonged to Hope for the Bereaved in Syracuse for many years after the loss of my husband. I volunteered in various capacities. Each person who entered grief counseling had a story of their personal transition from loss. One of the features many in the support group identified with was a garden Hope for the Bereaved started in 1990 located in Liverpool, NY. In a way to acknowledge their grief, bricks were inscribed with the names and dates of their loved ones and placed in a curving path shaped like a butterfly, a symbol of hope. This way they could visit and honor them in a colorful garden display as well as a yearly memorial celebration.

My idea was encouraged by observing how my German friend went through her grieving process, solemnly. In Germany loved ones are buried in church yards dedicated to family members. Although there was a ceremony around the burial process, often-times, grievers had lost momentum to visit the bare cemetery plots at churchyards. During my time in Germany with Christiana, we went to many gardens with colorful displays of flowers and monuments in public parks. As I thought more about my idea I proposed it to my friend Susan. She encouraged me to start the application process for the contest. Again, I had a sensation I was meant to return to Germany.

I worked on writing about having a similar garden in many of the public parks. I wrote about how others faced adversity in their life after a loss, especially death. During the transition, many use their grief to create something that might help others. Facing adversity often strengthens our resolve to deal with loss. Entering this contest would be another way for me to transition, too. Although it took a few months after I submitted my application along with pictures, I heard from the foundation.

I visited the Ukrainian National Home in Syracuse on St. Patrick's Day after a parade. When I returned home a letter with a return address from Germany was in the mailbox. I quickly opened it. I could understand most of the message, but the next day I visited my German friend.

Christiana said, "Your transition idea was accepted. You should make arrangements compliments of Korber Foundation for a flight and hotel in Potsdam, Germany. Make sure your arrival date coincides with the other contestants and staff from the Korber Foundation."

My other friend, Susan, who collaborated with me on the project was also invited. When I called her to share about winning, she responded, "Oh my, that is so wonderful. Can we travel together?"

I responded, "Certainly, we can stay at the same hotel. I'll make the plans."

In the late summer, we finally arrived in the village of Potsdam, Germany. I heard Ukrainian music in a courtyard near the hotel when I got out of the cab. When I went into the hotel to receive my room arrangement, I asked, "What is the musical display?"

The attendant said, "Oh, the whole month of August is reserved to honor the Ukrainian soccer team for their first induction into the World Cup soccer tournament in 2006."

For the next few days, I experienced an odd connection to my late husband. He was somehow near me although in a metaphysical nature.

I was affirmed of that energy field when the Korber staff brought our group of fifteen to an exclusive resort near a lake outside Potsdam. When we arrived at the resort, I spotted a large bus in the parking lot. It was blue and yellow like the Ukrainian flag. In large letters across the side of the bus was written Ukrainian Soccer Team. I was comforted knowing I was in this place at another coincidental time. After a few days of celebrating the group's victory, I met the soccer team. I spoke in Ukrainian to make a connection.

One man asked, "Where are you from?"

"I am from the United States."

After we exchanged travel stories many of them gave me their autographs. Later, when I returned home I donated the autographs to the Syracuse Ukrainian National Home for a fundraiser.

As a final tribute to the group, we were escorted to Berlin and honored by various international ambassadors at the Mozart concert hall. Each individual from the group went on stage for an award that recognized their idea for Germany from their country. There were fifteen new ideas adopted that day. "Latchkey Children from the US," "Transitions From School Settings," and "Scientific Research" were just a few.

After the elaborate ceremony was over, the group said their goodbyes and went on their way home. I had extra time to visit the city of Berlin and some historical buildings. During my walk, I came across a memorial museum that honored the many Jews who were killed during WWII. Set in a courtyard not far from the Brandenburg gate, small cafes, and stores, I walked the curved undulating path that led to an underground museum. Once inside, I viewed various displays representing other cultural groups who also lost their lives in the war.

Behind glass window displays were bags, clothes, shoes, and suitcases that had been scattered objects in small villages that had been destroyed. These remnants of the past introduced me to another viewpoint and the struggles of humanity. This experience caused me emotional pain facing a reality I had only learned about from my husband's family who survived that time period. All these new insights expanded the complexities of war. I was disturbed yet moved as if I was in a twilight zone of grief I had been in for years, although an enlightening experience.

Marrying this Ukrainian immigrant was one of the most exciting experiences in my life. We were able to create a dual-culture relationship as we looked more sincerely into what is important when you love someone. "Only the heart knows what the mind cannot comprehend," as Kahil Gibran, the Prophet so eloquently writes about. It takes effort to confront the differences of opinions in the intellect and heart. My husband and I did that until his death. Then the transition of my life went on a different path.

As I review my past, I look at it as a period of learning various languages and cultural traditions with those I became involved with over the years, creating a sense of connection, and consider myself very fortunate. All those nations' values and belief systems affected my own viewpoint. Although the gravitational pull I experienced throughout my years often sensed I was in a liminal state of being during the grief process, I realize now that my journey was not as much physical as it was metaphysical. What a great journey even from my hometown, Syracuse, as I encountered intellectual change.

All the years that brought me out of the '60s and '70s to a new worldview were a rewarding experience. Although the continuing crisis in our world affairs has not diminished much since that time period, peace is still the best option to embrace shared ethnic harmony. Every generation has a part to play on this world stage in large or small ways as we go about our individual journeys.

22

A New Life

Sylvia O'Connor

On January 1, 1990, at 4 a.m., I felt invaded and possessed. The crystal ball of my life shattered; there would be no going back to that safe, wonderful path. I would be lost in a nightmarish wilderness for seven years before finding out what was happening to me.

I didn't jump up on New Year's morning and make a delicious breakfast like I'd planned. All my bones and muscles felt abused. Something was wrong. I knew it as surely as a warning tattooed to the back of my hand. I lay in bed lethargic, stiff and sore, full of fear and heaviness, and let Dennis get up with the girls. They were downstairs. I could hear him talking, the coffee brewing in the old percolator, and the girls chattering as they ran back and forth to the dining room to set the table. Soon, I could smell the bacon and coffee, and yet I wasn't jumping out of bed.

"Hey Syl, breakfast," Dennis called.

"Okay," I shouted back.

I fought through the terrifying fatigue and shuffled to the bathroom in the same doddering way as during the night. I wasn't as wobbly and rather than stagger I could walk a straight line. At the top of the stairs, however, I hesitated, unsure how to take my unstable body down them.

Finally, I clung to the banister with both hands and eased one foot down at a time. This must be what old people feel like, I thought. My muscles felt too weak to hold the baby in, and my shins itched like poison ivy will. A grim portend of doom befell me, and as soon as I descended and shuffled my way to the couch, I stayed put.

Dennis brought over bacon and eggs, toast and orange juice, which I ate half-sitting. Calling the doctor on New Year's Day would be futile, so we decided to take it easy and phone him in the morning. Cailin, Tara, and Lauren hung around me with their workbooks and coloring books, talking and showing me their pictures, but I was distracted, my mind on myself and the baby.

During the three previous pregnancies, the final trimesters were joyous times of energy and expectation. I had napped and trips to the bathroom kept me up at night, but this tiredness made my heart pound, like being sucked into a place with extra gravitational pull. This has to be fatigue, I thought. It was bone-deep like nothing I'd felt before. "Easy there, girl," I told myself.

As we walked from the parking lot to Dr. Watson's office, I slipped both hands under my belly to support it. "Lauren," I said, "I want you to hold onto Tara's hand and not let go. Can you do that?" She nodded and took Tara's hand. The parking lot was too big and formidable for an impulsive two-year-old, even one as smart and capable as Lauren.

"Lauren," I said, "if you hold Tara's hand all the way across this parking lot, I will buy you a piece of candy—understand?" Lauren bobbed her head up and down several times.

With Dennis at work and my children next to me, I thought back on when I was first referred to Dr. Watson. "He will deliver you lying on his back if that's what you want," somebody told me about him. I wanted to go natural with this baby and to use the birthing place at St. Joseph's Hospital, which simulated a home birth by having a wallpapered room and a king-sized bed. You could have your children present and a midwife, which is what I'd decided to do.

Dr. Watson was tall and handsome with long limbs, dark hair, and a pleasant casualness that ensured trust. He was also kid-friendly and could make a big sister-to-be feel very much a part of "her" baby coming. I lay on the examining table, pulled up my shirt, and told him about feeling paralyzed, which I obviously wasn't.

I said, "Something feels wrong inside me, like this baby is going to fall out when I stand up. It's scaring me!"

"That's common. The more babies a woman has the more afraid she becomes." Dr. Watson squeezed clear goo over my stretched belly and slid the sonogram wand back and forth until a rapid clip of heartbeat sounded.

"That's your baby's heartbeat," he said grinning down at Lauren and Tara. Tara stared up at him with big, somber eyes and didn't say anything. Lauren started to whine, anxious for her candy. I pointed out the rash on my shins and the top of my feet.

"We don't worry about rashes. All kinds of rashes are common with pregnancy. That will go away after the baby is born."

"But something is wrong!" I insisted. "It feels like I'm going to miscarry and I'm way beyond tired for this late in the pregnancy. I can hardly get up out of bed!"

Dr. Watson eased toward the door until his hand reached the doorknob. When a doctor's hand is on the doorknob the appointment is over, I knew that.

"Don't worry," he said, "everything is okay."

In a panic, I started to cry. "But something is wrong, I'm sure of it!"

He slipped out quickly, pulling the door closed behind him.

It was the first door of many to be closed by doctors. I came to know the gesture as a patent formula for dismissal. Using the gown, I wiped my eyes and then the gel from my belly.

"Don't cry Mommy," Tara said tearfully, while Lauren hugged my leg. As I ushered them out the door, bitter distrust burned in my throat. I'm not a panicky type or a whiner either, and I think I know my own body, I thought.

During the drive home, however, I reconsidered the visit from the doctor's perspective. What was he to do after all? My cervix was closed. Babies don't just fall out. And fatigue wasn't something he could actually see. As I passed Wegmans and took the right-hand lane onto Route 92 toward Manlius I concluded, "You need to do what feels right in your own body. You will have to take care of yourself."

As a unit manager in Boone County Hospital in Missouri, I'd seen people put their whole trust in doctors. I saw it as a mistake. Doctors sometimes act like gods, but they're not. They are "practicing" medicine; trained to make quick, educated decisions, or guesses in ambiguous situations based on experience. They are not all knowing.

At home, I lay on the couch. I was not going to have a premature birth if I could help it. During meal-making, I reeled with weakness and fatigue. I made the easiest, fastest meals then lay right back down. It put a greater burden of work on Dennis' shoulders, but that's the way it would have to be. Dennis always said, "Who said life was easy?" Well, it wasn't easy for either of us as Carolyn's birth grew closer.

Some days fatigue drifted over me. Sometimes it lifted. The rash on my shins bubbled like an orange peel at first, then grew dark and ugly. I wore long pants whenever I went out. The itching was intense and I scratched every time I wasn't paying attention.

At subsequent appointments, I grew more insistent. "This reeling tiredness must be fatigue. It feels unnatural."

"I don't have an answer for that but look at all the work you're doing with three young kids," Dr. Watson teased. Then he repeated what he'd said before: "The more pregnancies a woman has the more she worries."

The kids can come to the birthing center if the parents agree to it. That idea settled in my belly like a weight. They would have to watch a birth tape, a video of four mothers giving birth naturally, one after the other. At home, I plugged it into the VCR.

The girls sat spellbound in a semicircle on the floor in front of the television set and didn't make a peep. The camera zoomed in on the labia as it stretched apart to reveal a tiny circle of the baby's head. Grunting and pushing were followed by cries and moans as the mother pushed the baby out a little more. The girls leaned into one another and held their breaths. They held hands, their little bodies tense with excitement. Finally, a liver-colored, reddish-blue baby rushed out all wet and slippery. It looked HUGE and was covered in creamy, wax-like vernix. The girls rolled onto their backs and around on the floor squealing in a pandemonium of delight. Sometimes I watched with a few thoughts of my own: What have I set myself up for by bringing this tape home? Why hadn't I been shown a video like this before giving birth myself?

They saw forty births, or more correctly, the same four births ten times, and each time they remained riveted to the TV. Every day Cailin said, "Mom, please don't let me miss this."

"I don't know, Cailin," I said. Every time I considered all the pushing I would have to do to birth a baby and glanced at Cailin, I had to turn away.

"Mom, I really, really, really want to be there for this!" She took my hands in hers and looked up at me with big, pleading eyes. "Mom, please," she said, "pleaseeee don't let me miss this!"

Still, I wasn't sure. To have a child in the birthing room you had to have someone other than the father there to watch the child. I asked my good friend Liz, who said, "Oh, Syl, I would love to be there. Call me—day or night."

The day Carolyn was born, Cailin came home from school and fell soundly asleep. She slept right through dinner, and then on through the evening. I thought about waking and feeding her before bed, but finally, I didn't.

At two in the morning, I called Liz, "We're on our way!" Cailin popped awake still fully dressed. Our neighbor, who was on call to watch the younger two, rushed in as we headed for the door. Getting to the hospital in a timely fashion was the one thing on my mind. "You are coming, Cailin. Stay here with Mr. Ringwood until Liz gets here." I quickly kissed her and closed the door.

The monitor strapped to my belly was making a de-lump-de-lump-de-lump galloping sound when Liz and Cailin arrived. I lay back while Liz and Dennis cracked jokes and Cailin galloped around the room to the music of the baby's heartbeat. I couldn't help laughing between contractions. It was a birthing party with a nurse, a midwife, Dennis, Liz, Cailin and me.

The midwife and nurses tried to hurry the delivery along. A baby comes when it is ready and a mother's body will tell her when to push with an impulse so strong that they can say don't push and she will push her brains out anyway. I knew that from experience. This time, with all their urging, I tried pushing and all that came out was a little poop. I refused to push again until a few minutes later when my body said to push.

When Carolyn eased out, Dennis' hands, Liz's hands, and the midwife's were all there to catch her. The lights were low for the baby's eyes and I could smell amniotic fluid. Dennis climbed into bed, held Carolyn against his bare chest with one arm and pulled Cailin up with the other. They peered down at the new baby with the softest expressions. "Look Cailin," Dennis whispered, "it's little Carolyn."

"Oh, little Carolyn," Cailin said and her face glowed with a relaxed joyousness I'd never seen before on a child.

Dennis rocked the baby back and forth and softly said, "People would pay millions for a baby like this." Eventually, Cailin would tell Carolyn, "I knew you from the minute you were born."

After Carolyn's birth, I didn't get better, and it always seemed prophetic or biblical that I should lose the life I was living on the first day of a new year and decade. The fatigue lessened and worsened, good days and bad days, and when I walked the easy three-block slope from the library to our house, it felt like a rough hand squeezed my heart.

23

EVERYBODY DOWN

KIMBERLY PARR

I grew up in a leafy Maryland suburb outside Washington, D.C., where nothing much happened until a few days before Easter in 1975. That's when two sisters walked to our local shopping center for a slice of pizza and vanished without a trace.

Katherine and Sheila Lyon were 10 and 12 years old, respectively. I had just turned 13 and my sister Dede was 11. We had walked to Wheaton Plaza many times without adult supervision. It was a sunny, open-air shopping center with restaurants, shoe stores, record shops, and a movie theater. At Easter, there was the added attraction of holiday decorations, including a giant rabbit that talked and dispensed jellybeans from its paw. Several people, including the girls' brother, recalled seeing them that day, sharing a slice of pizza, and having fun.

Then, they were gone. No one had witnessed an abduction or heard a scream. There were no signs of a struggle. They just never came home.

Hundreds of police officers and volunteers searched woods, ponds, sewers, and vacant lots around their Kensington neighborhood. Detectives interviewed and cleared dozens of potential suspects. Days passed with no break in the investigation, and the region slowly slipped into shock. It was unfathomable. How could two blond sisters simply vanish from a suburban shopping center in broad daylight?

Undated photos of Katherine and Sheila Lyon released by the Federal Bureau of Investigation (FBI). The girls vanished from a Wheaton, Maryland, shopping center on March 25, 1975.

But they had. Six months after Katherine and Sheila disappeared, the biggest criminal investigation in Montgomery County history quietly folded. No trace of them was ever found.

The Lyon sisters' disappearance haunts me to this day. Those of us who lived through it never got over it. Even as children, we knew something monstrous and unspeakable had happened. For decades, I couldn't think of them without a shiver of horror.

That's probably why, 38 years later, while living in Syracuse, New York, I sat up and took notice during a cable TV news show, *Your Haunted Hometown*. A husky, middle-aged man was standing next to the Erie Canal in Chittenango, 15 miles east of Syracuse, and talking about another child who had vanished without a trace. It was a wild, weirdly credible story involving predatory kids, a hasty burial, a deathbed confession, and the possibility that, nearly a century later, a young boy was entombed under a decayed canal boat.

This was juicy stuff. I hopped on the Internet and found a single description of a Chittenango area "Ghost Hunt" promising, among other things, to treat visitors to the tale of a young boy who "accidentally died from jumping off a bridge." That was it. No missing person reports, no cold-case updates, and no discovery of an unidentified child's remains in the canal. The kid, if he existed at all, was just a stop on a haunted history tour, a ghost in the water.

The kid, I thought, deserved better.

Years passed. I left my public relations job for a civil service position with New York State, moved to the suburbs, and thought occasionally about the boy under the boat. Someone should go after him, I'd say to myself. And, Someone should look into this. It was beginning to dawn on me that maybe that someone should be me. But I had a husband, a child, a full schedule, and a busy job. Time was a resource I definitely did not have.

Then COVID slammed into New York State. On March 16, 2020, my employer sent everyone home until further notice. Suddenly, I had time to spare. What better way to use it than to get to the bottom of this strange story that had nagged at me since I'd watched Your Haunted Hometown? Maybe I could determine the child's identity. Maybe I would even write about it.

I Googled with renewed vigor. There were a couple of new references to paranormal investigations in Chittenango, but nothing indicating the crime had ever been formally investigated. I managed to find, and rewatch, the original TV news show from 2013, and learned the name of the man I saw interviewed: Doug Rainbow. He was a former police investigator and Co-Founder of the Chittenango Landing Canal Boat Museum, a six-acre site featuring an excavated, 19th-century dry dock just yards from where the deadly incident allegedly occurred. Was he still alive? I wondered.

He was. Five days later, I cold-called Doug Rainbow.

* * *

The village of Chittenango, population 5,000, lies between the northern edge of the Allegheny Plateau and the Ontario Lowlands in Central New York. It takes its name from the creek the native Haudenosaunee (Iroquois) people called Chu-de-nääng, a 55-mile-long tributary that plunges over a spectacular, 167-foot waterfall before winding through the center of town. The name roughly translates to, "Where the waters divide and run north."

One mile north of the village lies the Old Erie Canal, the artificial waterway that once ran for 363 miles from Albany to Buffalo. Just four feet deep and 40 feet wide when first hacked through the wilderness, the canal dramatically reduced travel time for both people and cargo, spurred economic development, enabled western expansion, brought unimaginable prosperity to settlements along its banks, and became a conduit for radical ideas about religion, social justice, and the rights of women. It also inspired a song still trilled by generations of American schoolchildren:

> *Low bridge, everybody down*
> *Low bridge, 'cause we're comin' to a town*
> *You'll always know your neighbor, you'll always know your pal*
> *If you've ever navigated on the Erie Canal.*

From the start, the Erie Canal was awash in weirdness.

In 1818, laborers digging out the canal through Chittenango unearthed the remains of a baby wooly mammoth. They quickly confiscated most of the skeleton for themselves, leaving only part of a tusk and lower jaw. The remains of the "Chittenango Mammoth," estimated to be around 13,000 years old, are now housed at the New York State Museum in Albany.

In 1832, a wave of cholera swept up from New York City, spread by water contaminated by human feces. Following the practice of the day, canal travelers emptied their chamber pots overboard and unwittingly infected hundreds of people in the towns they'd just passed through. As the body count increased, wealthier citizens panicked and fled to the countryside, resulting in outbreaks miles from the canal. Today, dozens of victims of the cholera epidemic in Chittenango lie in unmarked graves just north of the canal on a knoll once known as Cholera Hill.

In addition to a dry dock, Chittenango Landing was also at times home to a sawmill, blacksmith, general store, and canning factory. Industrial accidents were common. An unnamed laborer boring out a pump log in 1850 was killed when a fly-wheel malfunctioned, sending a 60-pound piece of lead flying into his face. On April 2, 1906, Edward Diefendorf, Jr., 27, was repairing a boiler at Chittenango Landing when it suddenly exploded. The 500-lb. boiler blasted through a wall, flew more than 50 feet through the air, and landed in a tree, along with part of Diefendorf's body. Three other men were killed, but miraculously, the worker standing directly next to the boiler was uninjured. Diefendorf left a pregnant wife and three children. His head was never found.

The Erie Canal officially closed in 1917, but that didn't put an end to the weirdness. Visitors to the abandoned dry dock told of hearing a blacksmith's hammer striking an anvil, or the tolling of a faraway bell. Some swore they saw a candle flickering in the early-morning mist, carried by an unknown hand. Who was the woman in white who sometimes appeared on the towpath before fading from view? Was she the same entity who spooked the horse of a sheriff's deputy in the 1870s, causing both to fall into the canal and drown?

And what exactly was it about Chittenango that made it such a magnet for the strange, the deadly, the impossible-to-explain? Could its location at the geographic center of New York State have something to do with it? Was it karmic retribution wrought on behalf of the Haudenosaunee people dispossessed of their ancestral lands piece by piece? Perhaps Nature herself was rebelling at the felling of her forests, draining of her wetlands, and polluting of her waterways.

Whatever the reason, the village has maintained a reputation for weirdness, as I would learn following my first conversation with Doug Rainbow at the beginning of the COVID lockdown.

It was awkward, explaining why a stranger was reaching out more than six years after his appearance on Your Haunted Hometown, with questions about an alleged homicide that happened a hundred years ago on the Erie Canal.

"I'm a writer," I explained, "and I find the whole story fascinating. Do you remember giving that interview?"

"I've given lots of interviews," he growled.

I pressed on. "Do you believe a boy died after being pushed from the bridge at Chittenango Landing?"

"Yep."

"Do you think the body is still there? In the canal?"

"Probably."

"Was the death ever formally investigated?"

"Nope."

The sluice gates suddenly broke open. "I know the story is true," he said, his flat, wary responses giving way to complete sentences. "An old friend called and asked me to meet her at the canal. She said her brother just died and she had something important to tell me. We'd been friends for decades, so of course I said yes."

Then Doug Rainbow unspooled the story told to him by a friend hoping to right the wrong done to a child passing through Chittenango so long ago.

"Her brother met her at the canal and told her that when he was a kid in the 1920s, he and a friend were playing on the high bridge that used to span the canal. A strange boy came along, someone from out of town, and they goaded him into jumping off the bridge."

He cleared his throat and continued.

"There wasn't much water in the canal at the time," he said. "The kid landed head-first and got stuck in the mud. The other two ran down and pulled him out, and he was dead. An abandoned boat was tied up nearby, and they buried him in the mud between the boat and the wall. Probably used a plank from the boat to dig the hole. He told his sister he'd just learned he was dying of cancer and wanted to go out with a clean slate. He pointed out where everything had happened, then died two weeks later. She pointed out everything to me. Then she died two weeks later."

He said he had been a police investigator for 32 years, and based on his training, he believed the boy was pushed.

"If he had jumped, he'd have landed feet-first," he growled. "And the other kids would've run for help, but that's not what happened. It wasn't an accident, but it wasn't murder, either. It was just a stupid prank gone wrong."

He was able to tell me the name of his friend—I'll call her "Melanie"—but little else. Who was Melanie's brother, the one who did the pushing? He didn't know. When did it happen? Prior to 1927, because that's when the State tore down all the high bridges over the canal and replaced them with concrete culverts at street level. Who was the second boy on the bridge, the one who helped bury the body? According to the brother, he died as a teen in a fireworks accident.

I had one more question. "Why," I asked, "did Melanie die just two weeks after their meeting at Chittenango Landing?"

He sighed. "I have no clue," he said. "She seemed perfectly fine."

* * *

A lot has happened since I made that first phone call to Doug Rainbow in March of 2020.

I was able to quickly identify the brother who confessed and interview his surviving relatives, now in their 70s and 80s. None of them seemed to be at all troubled by the possibility that their father/uncle may have committed a serious crime. They were each happy to dish, sharing family stories both harrowing and poignant.

It took longer to identify the second boy on the bridge. I discovered he was an orphan, having already lost one parent to murder in a speakeasy brawl over whiskey, and another to strep throat. He died of lockjaw (tetanus poisoning) at 13 following a fireworks accident, a not-uncommon occurrence at the time. Life in 1920s rural America, I was learning, was occasionally nasty, frequently brutish, and often quite short.

Doug Rainbow died in October of 2021, but not before we met with three New York State Police investigators at Chittenango Landing. They peered into the water, walked up and down, took measurements, and then told us since everyone involved was dead, they couldn't declare the site a crime scene. Investigation over... for now.

There have been false starts, dead ends, bombshell revelations, and a second, stunning confession. Family and friends think I'm obsessed, and of course, they're right. Yet the story has an undeniable ring of truth that grows louder with each passing year, mainly because of the questions raised if it isn't true:

Why would a dying man confess to a crime he didn't commit?

Why would a loving sister make up a story about her late brother?

Why would a former police investigator concoct a yarn that could be easily disproved by peeking under a now-decayed canal boat?

And ... why do I care?

I wasn't just looking for a ghost in the water. I was trying to right a wrong. But which one?

While researching the Erie Canal, I became fascinated with the word "mudlark," a 19th-century expression for a boat that had run aground. Mudlarking could happen suddenly, such as during an embankment collapse, when boats upstream might find themselves helplessly swept toward the breach until they hit bottom. Or it could happen gradually, as in late autumn, when the Erie Canal was drained before the first hard freeze, and boat owners simply allowed their craft to mudlark nearby where they could keep an eye on them through the winter.

Regardless of how exactly one came to be mudlarked, the outcome was the same: You were stuck until you were unstuck. It was supposed to be a temporary state. But when the Old Erie Canal closed for good in 1917, hundreds of boats from Albany to Buffalo were permanently mudlarked, abandoned to decay, and sink in place.

I came to realize the people tied to the tragedy at Chittenango Landing were each mudlarked in their own way. Melanie's brother, never quite free of the act he committed as a child, revisited it decades later once he realized a reckoning was at hand. The friend with him on the bridge that day, named for an uncle killed in a freak accident on the canal, abandoned by an alcoholic father, and orphaned at 13, seemed doomed to die young. And nearly a century after he was pushed from a bridge over the Erie Canal, an anonymous child likely remains entombed under a sunken steam barge.

I, too, am mudlarked, haunted by a tragedy that claimed two sisters and shattered my innocence almost 50 years ago. It wasn't just a missing boy I was seeking. It was the part of me that went missing in the spring of '75 when I slipped from childhood to adolescence in the shadow of an unspeakable crime.

Abandoned steamboat at Chittenango Landing, circa 1920. Photo courtesy of Chittenango Landing Canal Boat Museum, used with permission.

24

LIGHTNING STRUCK TWICE

AARON M. PERRINE

The second house my parents owned was struck by lightning. It was the second house that I had lived in, from age three until I left for college.

Morning or evening, I don't know, but I remember my father telling me weeks after it struck that it had hit the chimney and followed that down and that it moved on to the living room wall adjacent to the chimney. That wall was opposite the large windows that individually made up the most striking feature of the home. The tremendous amount of electricity was partially conducted through the wallpaper's foil backing and charred the wall. I don't remember the wallpaper pre- or post-strike; blue and yellow stripes come to mind.

My father is gone—I no longer can ask him. My mother is still here, but I didn't ask her about it.

My father was gone the day or night of the lightning strike, too—a business trip to Singapore or England. I still have a carved elephant and a Metropolitan Police whistle he got me from those frequently visited destinations. I don't remember whether or not it was that specific trip that he brought me the elephant or the whistle. The elephant sits on my desk; I gave my son the whistle the day of my father's funeral, a little less than two years ago. I still had the box it came in.

In addition to the scorched wallpaper, the lightning blasted a roundish hole in the plaster wall above the door in my brother's room, dead-centered horizontally and vertically. The white of the shattered plaster on the floor was confusing to me; I might have been five or six. I understood the wall was painted, but I think I thought that wall paint was more like dye, even though I had painted pictures in art class at school and had frequently made a mess with watercolors at home. I then realized that paint largely sat on a surface, stuck fast to it. Maybe I thought the wall would be like the scrap paper I used for watercolors then—soaked through.

During the pandemic, author and illustrator Mo Willems shot a video series titled Lunch Doodles to entertain children who weren't attending school. My son, inspired, made marker drawings of monsters with huge blue eyes after he returned to school for third grade. They were done on high-quality marker paper that does not allow the ink to soak through. One of them sits on my desk today.

My third-grade teacher had an upright piano in his classroom. The finish was darkened from age; dust and whitened varnish had accumulated in the crevices of the ornamentation. It had the player mechanicals in it once, but as I think about it today that doesn't seem right—it might not have once been a player piano at all. My godmother—my mother's best friend from childhood—did have an upright player piano in her parlor, long inoperable; I recall the brass levers just in front of the keys that adjusted certain parameters of the making of music. I tried to look up what these levers did specifically; Player Piano Servicing and Rebuilding by Arthur Reblitz is a highly recommended guide to player pianos, according to what I could find online—but I also found out what those levers did depends on which brand of piano it was.[1] If I once knew what brand of piano it was, I long since have forgotten.

My third grade had a morning meeting with the class across the hall; they would shuffle over and my teacher would play that non-player piano. He was a skilled amateur pianist—my father's phrase for those who didn't pursue music professionally, but he felt were talented.

The meeting always included singing "This Is Just A Happy Song," an Up With People tune, which I loved. [2] It is possible that we didn't sing it all that often, but I loved it so much that I wished it to be that way.

One morning meeting I played that piano. I remember the basic outline of the piece, but not the title or how to play it; it was a series of arpeggiated chords. The arpeggios progressed through the octaves from low to high. There was a fermata at the end, damper pedal down, dampers up. The chord changed, and the progression would begin again. In one phrase, I repeated an arpeggio one too many times and went too high, according to the sheet music. I stopped, mid-performance, turned to my right slightly, toward the back of the room, using the round swivel stool, and said to the class, "That was one too many."

Meeting over, my teacher admonished: "Nobody knew that you made a mistake until you mentioned it."

---

1. Reblitz, Arthur A. Player Piano Servicing & Rebuilding: A Treatise on How Player Pianos Function, and How to Get Them Back into Top Playing Condition If They Don't Work. Vestal Press, 1993.

2. Allen, Jane. Just A Happy Song, Musicnotes, ww.musicnotes.com/sheetmusic/mtd.asp?ppn=MN0049218. Accessed 15 Jan. 2024.

He would not like for me to say this—especially not using his own phrase—but another skilled amateur pianist of my childhood was my father; his copy of Everybody's Favorite Community Songs [3] is a treasury of outdated popular musical culture; many of the songs within were over 25 years old when it was copyrighted in 1935. In addition, the book contained some much older material; of those, "The Old Oaken Bucket" was a favorite of ours.

I later learned that in addition to learning about this music by playing from that songbook, he was knowledgeable about the music of these eras because there had been an abandoned Edison cylinder record player, with a number of records, in a dilapidated house his father had rented. My father told me once that he could remember the shape formed by the cracked plaster above his bed in one of those houses.

If you research "The Old Oaken Bucket" today, you'll discover that it was included in many temperance songbooks, lines like the following were designed to influence the inebriates of the 1800s to renounce drink and just drink waters: [4][5]

then soon, with the emblem of truth overflowing,
And dripping with coolness, it rose from the well [6]

---

3. Everybody's Favorite Community Songs. Amsco Music Sales Co., 1935.

4. Ewing, George W. "The Well-Tempered Lyre." Southwest Review, vol. 56, no. 2, spring 1971, pp. 139–155.

5. "The Old Oaken Bucket." Mutopia Project, www.mutopiaproject.org/cgibin/piece-info.cgi?id=436. Accessed 15 Jan. 2024.

6. "The Old Oaken Bucket." Mutopia Project, www.mutopiaproject.org/cgibin/piece-info.cgi?id=436. Accessed 15 Jan. 2024.

I was horrified by this fact when I unearthed it—the connection between me, my father, and the song seemed to be severed by it being used instrumentally:

The cot of my father
The dairyhouse nigh it
And e'en the rude bucket
that hung in the well. [7]

I wanted those words to be from a song about memory and the relative innocence of childhood, for them to only have intrinsic value. A few copies of Everybody's Favorite Community Songs are listed for sale on Abebooks for a few dollars; my copy, repaired many times, sits on my desk; there's a homemade buttonhook that belonged to my father in it to mark a page.

I was near a lightning strike again—I was about 12, and observing a thunderstorm from my maternal grandparents' front porch. An old tree in the setback from their small-city street exploded with violence that is not easily described. The noise was tremendous. The tree didn't fall.

A story I had heard when I was a child was that Will Dillon—Cortland, New York native, vaudeville performer, and lyricist of "I Want a Girl (Just Like The Girl That Married Dear Old Dad)"—had lived in my grandparent's house, my mother's childhood home. As an adult, I discovered it was one of Will's many brothers who had owned the house, and not even one of the ones who performed in vaudeville with him. [8] My mother, who kept

---

7. "The Old Oaken Bucket." Mutopia Project, www.mutopiaproject.org/cgibin/piece-info.cgi?id=436. Accessed 15 Jan. 2024.

8. Dabes, Ruth. "Man of a Thousand Songs." The Rotarian, May 1953, pp. 39–60.

(and still keeps) seemingly everything, inherited the abstract for her childhood home, so I could easily check who had owned it.

In later life, Dillon was a dedicated member of Rotary, and the May 1953 issue of The Rotarian recounts the story of him leaving Cortland for Boston and show business. His parents had wanted him to go to prep school in Ithaca and then attend Cornell University. A man was hired to take his trunk to the Lehigh Valley railroad station (and Ithaca). Dillon instead directed the man to take it to the Delaware, Lackawanna & Western station.[9]

The article in The Rotarian does not detail which station Dillon was to depart from in his parent's idealistic vision of his future, nor which one he told the porter to go to instead; I pieced that together from local knowledge and his mentioning that he switched departing stations. You could take either railroad north to connect to points east, but the Lackawanna did not serve Ithaca directly from Cortland, as the Lehigh Valley did.

How moving to me it would have been if the story of Will Dillon living in my grandparents' house were true, and he had left the house my mother and I knew, looked east briefly, and saw the tree that later was killed by lightning before turning west toward the train station that was close to my grandparent's home, along the tracks where my mother played and I had played. The tree was old in the mid-1980s when I was twelve; could it have been there in the mid-1890s? I am susceptible to that sort of romanticism; I then thought Dillon might have mentioned this to the interviewer, who then chose to not include it.

The epigraph in James Salter's last novel *All That Is* reads, "There comes a time when you realize that everything is a dream,

---

9. Dabes, Ruth. "Man of a Thousand Songs." The Rotarian, May 1953, pp. 39–60.

and only those things preserved in writing have any possibility of being real."[10]

I realize Salter didn't mean to admonish us—write down everything!—he is clearly making points concerning the fallibility of memory, the impermanence of thought, the inevitability of death, and how we can try to ameliorate those fundamental facts about our lives, about human life. But it still feels to me like an admonishment from a writer who was very much more than a talented amateur.

I have puzzled so many times since the day I played the piano in morning meeting what can be safely improvised, and what can be made to seem well done by leaving something unsaid. One of the saddest parts of growing up for me was coming to the realization that it was not universally good to have a known path to take in a given situation because, for me, especially, maturity seemed to update my thinking. I had created those known paths solely to avoid embarrassment—which, of course, was the day I played the piano for my class.

I thought, while considering this piece, that the best way to evoke some parts of my childhood, and parts of me, was to tell about the odd coincidence that I was close to two lightning strikes, and how deeply embarrassed I was by what happened when I played the piano for my 3rd grade class. I quickly realized, though, that I didn't remember, didn't know, couldn't find out, and might be mistaken about so many of the details that I wanted to use to evoke my childhood that I became concerned that this piece just wouldn't work. The writerly solution is to simply reduce the amount of included detail, but I felt strongly I should resist that, maybe because it seemed too much like my teacher's solution to my musical mistake,

---

10. Salter, James. All That Is. Knopf, 2014.

and I so much wanted to be right about that day on that day, and I still want to be right about it, today.

I emphatically want to say that it is not always, but generally, better to put in too much and give too much than to withhold too much and keep too much, but just as quickly as I think it, "generally" transforms into a false note.

Something paraphrased from a textbook for my introductory college philosophy class is apt: gather ye rosebuds while ye may is great advice, but it leaves a vital question unanswered—which rosebuds?

To remind us of my father, and our saddest day of the past few years—perhaps the saddest day of his life—my son keeps the whistle I gave him on his desk, and I keep the box it came in on mine. It might also be a reminder to be moderate, and ultimately self-forgiving, when deciding what (and how) to write; what to keep and what to give away; what to tell and what to leave untold; and what to gather and what to pass over. It is not a possibility to play it all exactly right.

25

Doc's Dilemma

Lee B. Savidge

Fifty three degrees below zero outside and the Quonset hut's curved ribbed metal roof shudders, buffeted by harsh winds. Snowdrifts are piling up over the windows. Inside a rag-tag assortment of soldiers huddle around the battle-scarred but solid wooden table. The remaining cards from a deck are neatly stacked on the table next to the open beer can in front of the dealer. Most of the men have an open can or two perched at attention in front of them as they secretively eye one card at a time trying not to reveal their hand. The crew chief, a burly man with a booming voice, yells across the room at my father,

"C'mon Doc, it's poker night! Come join the game!"

The nearby radar tower, that pokes out of the Arctic snow, supports a giant dome shaped like a construction worker's hardhat without a brim. The winter storm's wind whistles and howls, drowning out the constant hum of the radar turning and the diesel generators groaning. The handy-crafted sign on the generator shed says, "Barter Island Power and Light Company, producer of Northern Lights." A similar sign on the nearby Quonset hut announces, "Welcome to Barter Island Waldorf Astoria." Someone has tacked a notice on the sign saying "Maids Wanted."

Half the men have scruffy beards they've been growing for months. Much of the furniture in the Quonset hut looks more like garage sale rejects than official government property. There's no sign of spit shine. No officer in the U.S. Air Force is interested in visiting this remote location above the Arctic Circle to pull a surprise inspection.

Beyond the white bear-shaped sign that says, "Polar Brrrr Club," Doc sits at an old upright piano. Some of the keys are out of tune, but the men enjoy his rendition of "Alley Cat." He had played in a band in Binghamton, New York, before responding to the WWII poster of Uncle Sam pointing a finger and saying, "I want you!" So his music repertoire is quite extensive, but "Alley Cat" is the tune he likes to play when reminiscing about his young wife, Marie, and ten-year-old son, Lee, back at McGuire AFB, New Jersey.

His thoughts flash back to the time he and Marie organized a picnic for the Veterans Of Foreign Wars (VFW). What fun they had together. He misses her cooking and can almost taste in his mind the meals she made with her secret spicy marinade.

A smile comes to his face as his flashback turns to the time he took Lee into a base hanger and explored the aircraft there. He visualizes how Lee's face lit up as Lee sat in the cockpit and pretended to fly the large cargo plane.

He wonders if he did or said something that pissed off his commander. Wouldn't one of the younger single men in the unit have been more suited to fill this twelve-month tour of remote isolated duty? On the other hand, he postulates, keeping the Barter Island Weather Station operating efficiently is a significant Cold War assignment requiring dedicated people who can be trusted to do whatever is necessary. Trained in both Weather Forecasting and Weather Electronics Maintenance, he has important specialty skills necessary for this mission. The periodic readings of arctic weather conditions he helps produce and relay to higher headquarters, and to northern airbases, help keep aircrews and passengers safe. His ego thus self-assuaged, he's able to cope.

His orders say "Sgt. Donald L. Savidge," but the men nicknamed him "Doc" based on the "Doc Savage Magazine," which had gained much popularity among the military. When he hears his nickname called again to join their weekly game, as they had done repeatedly over the last eight months, he reaches for his cigarette cantilevered on the piano's edge. There are burn marks from a hundred prior cigarettes that consumed themselves faster than the music being played. He leans back on his piano stool and the cigarette glow brightens as he inhales a long drag. He tilts his head back, opens his mouth, and his gentle puff sends a smoke ring swirling toward the shuddering ceiling. He stares through the ring, as if to seek...divine guidance.

He learned to play poker as a boy, despite his Methodist parents' aversion to gambling and smoking, and he was still an avid player when he met his wife, Marie. One day, not long after they were married, he came home from a game with his head hanging low. He had lost an entire month's pay. Marie was livid, until he promised never to play poker again. He had kept that promise for years...until now. No...he had had enough of their nagging.

"OK guys, deal me in."

The storm finally clears and they receive the eagerly anticipated radio message announcing the ETA of an inbound supply and mail flight, which happens every month or two, weather permitting. So they rush to the diesel-powered tank-treaded snowplows and quickly bulldoze an icy landing strip and mark the way with flares.

The cargo plane appears on the horizon like the black silhouette of a fat soaring hawk. Before long the sun glints off the shiny aluminum body and the plane skis approach the makeshift runway leaning back like duck's feet approaching a pond. As the plane makes its first bouncing contact with the runway, a tail fin on the stripped skeletal remains of a previously crashed plane is ominously visible in the background. The landing is bumpy and the men hold their breath until the plane slows to taxi speed. The crew chief swings two flashlights pivoting his forearms like metronome needles. The cargo plane follows his signals and stops at the designated loading area.

Doc drops into the mailbag a thick envelope.

Marie is shocked when she opens it and six hundred dollars in cash spills out. In 1955, that's enough money to buy a good used car. The enclosed love letter, among other things, says, "This is to make up for that miserable time when I lost a month's pay."

The men no longer pester Doc to join their game.[1]

---

1. An earlier version of "Doc's Dilemma" won awards at the local and national levels of the 2020 Veterans administration Creative Arts Competition.

26

THE FEDERAL-AID HIGHWAY ACT OF 1956 AND ME

JACQUELINE SCHMITT

I'm only an occasional visitor to Syracuse now. Work, marriage, and family took me to other places, or maybe it's more accurate to put it this way: I chose places to work, to live, to raise a family far from Syracuse. Yet something tugs me to return—I even moved back here three times. I was married here. My older children were born here, my youngest finished high school here. My hometown is like a burr under my saddle; even when I'm riding away, I have to stop to figure out what's prickly and making me uncomfortable, what doesn't fit, what causes the sky to tilt and the ground to crumble and wash away.

When I traveled to Syracuse in December I went to see my brother Derek. It was my first visit to his new house, built next to the one our parents built in 1965. His house overlooks the same broad valley but from a slightly different perspective. From his back deck, you can see farther south toward Tully Valley. My parents' deck faces due west, where U.S. Route 20 winds its way up from Onondaga past acres of apple orchards.

Both my parents and my brother built their new homes on former pastureland. When we first moved there, we could see a herd of cattle grazing across the road and corn grew just beyond our mowed grass. When Derek drove me back to the city that day last December, we took the old roads we used to take before Route 81 was finished. That highway is part of the vast interstate network built in the 1960s and '70s, concrete ribbons that tore cities apart and paved over playgrounds and neighborhoods. One of my mother's friends was a dairy farmer who lost his land when 81 rolled north of Syracuse.

"Bob wept over every cow that was sold," she said. "He knew them all by name."

My mother took Derek and me to visit their farm on one hot summer day. It must have been the early 1960s. The land was flat and wide open—great for planting and harvesting, but also great for plowing the concrete roadbed then under construction. The new highway to connect Canada with Pennsylvania would divide Bob's farm in half, permanently preventing the dairy herd from grazing in the pastures and then sauntering home for milking time.

The large, cool barn was far enough from the right-of-way to be spared. I think I saw a tractor and bales of hay, but were there cows in the stanchions or barnyard? I can't remember. Bob married my mother's best friend Harriet. They built a new, brick ranch house parallel to the highway. Bob used the profits from selling his land to start a new business selling insurance. He collected antique fire engines and Harriet decorated his office with weathered barn wood salvaged from other farms sold off for ranch houses and wider roads.

Like Harriet and Bob, my parents wanted to build a new house. When 81 tore through downtown Syracuse and made its dusty way south, they found their own acre and a half of former farmland. I remember their excitement about finding the lot, developing the plans, laying the foundation, and digging the well. The house would be finished in September. I would start 7th grade, my brother 3rd. We would ride the school bus. It was 1965.

When I visited my brother, we took the back roads we used to drive before 81 was constructed not to see the old farms or enjoy the rolling landscape, but because 81 is now in the process of being re-constructed, or in some places, completely de-constructed. The elevated road is now unsafe. The portion of the highway in downtown Syracuse will be removed and all through-traffic will be rerouted east through the suburbs.

That visit in December was my first view of the project. As we approached the city, I saw only one concrete pillar remaining from the sweeping overpass we used to cross daily. The familiar highway had sailed past the nursing home where both of our parents had died. Now bulldozers were pulling down the embankments that had supported the roadbed and dump trucks were carting the soil away.

Derek and I ate lunch that day in an Irish pub in our old neighborhood—a much fancier place than it was when we lived in the city. Our block of Herkimer Street, however, has seen few changes since the late 1950s. The towering American elms may be gone, the privet hedges smaller, but the one- and two-family frame houses are the same. The block still looks as tidy as it did when we moved in 1965, the grass trimmed and the neighborhood park maintained.

Our backyard overlooked Lewis Park, with playgrounds and ball fields between us and St. Brigid's Church and parochial school. In the summer crowds gathered for Little League, and in the winter the ball diamond iced over for skating. Every school day, Sisters in long, black habits shepherded uniformed children into the secrets of the Latin Mass. My neighbors who went to parochial school said the classrooms were very crowded and they had to buy their books.

I went to Porter, a public school, three blocks away. Three blocks in the other direction was Tipperary Hill, where Irish families lived next to Ukrainians and Russians. Polish classmates talked about their faraway cousins who lived where Communists forced children to work in factories. "The needle of her sewing machine went right through her finger," one of them breathlessly told me.

In public school, the day began with the Pledge of Allegiance and a Bible reading. We stood for the first and sat, heads bowed, for the second. My third-grade teacher usually read, "When I was a child, I spoke as a child, I understood as a child, I thought as a child," apparently the one passage she found that would cover the sensibilities of all faiths. Once a week our classes stopped for released-time religious instruction. Catholic children would stream to St. Patrick's, while we few Protestants stayed behind. For all I knew, there were more Catholics than anyone else in America. Even with all that diversity of language and culture and food and immigrant experience, every child in Porter School was white.

No one reason seemed to be the cause of our move out of Syracuse in 1965. My parents talked about how a new house would help my brother's asthma. The school district began to allow teachers, like my mother, to live outside the city. The auto plant where my father worked moved from downtown to former farmland in the eastern suburbs, and the new interstate highways made it quick and easy to get everywhere. Yet feeding it all, I feel now, was an urgency to get the move done in time for my brother and me to begin the school year in a new district.

In the early 1960s, there were 33 elementary schools in Syracuse. They were scattered throughout the city so that every child could walk. Most of us lived close enough to school to walk home for lunch.

Parents liked neighborhood schools. They were safe. They were close. Some parents had attended the same school to which their children now went. The schools were big enough for students to make friends with children beyond their block, but small enough for parents to rest assured that these new friends came from familiar homes and families.

So if each elementary school reflected the composition of its neighborhood, looking at the student body of the schools could tell us a lot about the neighbors we chose to live near. Out of 33 schools, 25 of them were like my school, Porter: all of the students were white. Two elementary schools were majority Negro, as the reports called them.

The schools in Syracuse segregated children by race because the neighborhoods were segregated by race. Nearly two-thirds of all the Black children in Syracuse attended two schools in one neighborhood, the 15th Ward, which in 1963 was bulldozed to build Route 81. After the dust cleared, the two schools remained but the neighborhood was gone.

The Syracuse City School District now faced two problems. One they had known for a while: tests revealed that the children in the majority-Black schools scored much lower than other Syracuse children in basic skills. Black parents had been demanding for several years to improve the quality of the neighborhood schools their children attended. School leaders replied that the low scores and the segregated buildings were not their fault.

"I don't accept the premise that racial imbalance creates any kind of missed opportunity," one board member said in 1963. "I don't think the school should accept responsibility for solving what is basically a housing problem."

Yet a year later housing was the school district's problem, since the construction of the interstate highway destroyed the neighborhood where most of the city's Black children lived. Displaced families moved into adjoining neighborhoods where the schools quickly became overcrowded. The formerly "Negro-majority" schools were closed. By now the state education department joined the Black parents in demanding that Syracuse comply with the law to provide good education in decent schools to all children. In March 1965 the school board voted to desegregate the city schools. Black children would be bused out of the districts where they lived. To ensure diversity, purely neighborhood schools would be no more.

Black parents won a legal victory to desegregate the schools within the district—ten years after the Supreme Court ruling in Brown v. Board of Education. White parents, however, had other laws on their side, laws that had been on the books for decades. In the 1930s the federal government established rules about who could get loans to buy or improve their homes. They took maps of already segregated neighborhoods and codified them. Neighborhoods where the maps said "Negroes or Italians" lived were "red-lined;" banks were not allowed to lend money there. People who lived in red-lined neighborhoods like the 15th Ward could never own their own homes. They rented in buildings that were inevitably substandard because the landlords who owned them could not borrow money to fix them up.

You can still see the echoes of those maps in Syracuse. The areas that were colored green or blue continue to be prosperous and well-kept. Both renters and homeowners live in areas that are colored yellow, indicating that the houses are less valuable. In the early 1960s, the "yellow-lined" neighborhoods were still all-white. The yellow-lined areas bordered the demolished, red-lined areas, and so that was where Black families moved when they were forced out of their homes that lay in the path of the interstate.

White families had other options. They had equity in the homes they owned. They had received a leg up to buy those homes not only from decades of legal segregation but also from programs like the G.I. Bill. The Interstate Highway Act cleared slums and farmland alike and families spread in all directions to spend their new money on new homes in new school districts. In 1965 my family was among them. That's why my parents felt such urgency to move by September. That was when the schools in Syracuse would be de-segregated, and everything would change.

The construction of the interstate highways promised a new, revitalized America, but those promises could last only as long as the life of the concrete that built them.

After decades of non-stop traffic, of snowplows spreading corrosive salt, of dripping water dissolving the concrete, and rusting the steel, the elevated highway was now too expensive to repair. The lanes were too narrow, and the exit ramps too short. Tear it down, state authorities decided. Move the road a few miles east around the city. Furthermore, the original funders—the U.S. Department of Transportation—now recognized the "environmental injustice" caused by the projects they started in the 1960s.

When this plan was announced, I had moved back to Syracuse. I lived less than a mile from the highway that would absorb the re-routed traffic. On some days I heard a distant rumble but smelled no fumes. This was nothing, I thought, compared to the families living in the Pioneer Homes, a 1930s housing project mere feet from the highway slated to be removed. Dust and fumes cascaded down onto clotheslines and playgrounds, and through the windows and doors of an elementary school that sat in the highway's shadow.

My suburban neighbors used the language of invasion to describe the proposed changes: "We moved out of the South Side to get away from that." The distance from where I lived to the housing project under the highway is six miles—barely a twenty-minute drive.

"They're more comfortable being with their own people," my neighbors said at community meetings. "They can't afford a car, so they have to live downtown." Did my neighbors not know that once 81 was built the grocery stores and banks fled as well? That the downtown stores where we used to shop were now expensive apartments? That the industries where city residents had been able to walk to work had decades before decamped to the wide-open spaces on the edge of the suburbs?

When I moved away from Syracuse, as I did again in 2020, I moved to places without history. Not without history in a literal sense, of course, but the history of all those communities where I lived was not my history. In my own version of "white flight," I lived in neighborhoods that could be prosperous or diverse or cultured and I would be merely a beneficiary of their history—I wouldn't know what they had been like before or what they had gone through to look like they did now. I would never feel the dis-ease in those places that I would feel in my own hometown where I could drive down a street or look at a map and see the past. It's not only that I remember those places the way they used to be when I was a child but that I see the poverty and prosperity, privilege, and racism that made my hometown what it was then and what it is now.

Every community in America shares that disease. Our troubled past binds us together as surely as the Constitution we continue to amend or the ideals that call us to come up higher. Wiser minds than mine remind us that we cannot build a common future without facing our common past. If we do that, even concrete highways can be torn up and high-flying overpasses torn down and dirt embankments carted away to the gentle farmlands from which they came.

27

One Egg or Two

Jackie Southard

"Okay, Ryan, it's your turn to pick the first book to read tonight," I said.

We read every evening after the boys bathed, brushed their teeth, and put their PJs on. I loved our bedtime stories and how the books spurred the imaginations of my sons, Ryan and Scott, especially now that they were six and four and their worlds had expanded beyond our home. We talked about anything that popped into their heads.

I sat in my rocking chair and watched the boys as they squatted in front of their bookshelf in their yellow Big Bird PJs, pulling their favorite books from the stack.

"Here, Mom," Scott said as both boys climbed onto my lap. I wrapped my arms around them and read about Max's adventures in *Where the Wild Things Are*. They wiggled as they settled in, and their bony bottoms cut into my thighs; I grimaced as I made slight adjustments to reduce the pain.

When Max arrived at the land of the Wild Things, both boys slid off and acted out what the creatures did. "They roared their terrible roar and gnashed their terrible teeth and rolled their terrible eyes and showed their terrible claws."

When we finished, Ryan said, "My book next, Mom." He handed me *Are You My Mother?* and both boys climbed back onto my lap. I began, "A mother bird sat on her egg. The egg jumped..."

"Mom," Ryan said.

"What, honey?"

"How do human mothers have babies? Where do they come from?" His question startled me, and I wasn't sure what to say. Then, I recalled an article that advised parents not to overthink their answers. Keep it simple and short. If they want more information, they will ask. So, I told the boys, "The baby comes from mommy's tummy."

"But how does it get there?" Scott asked.

"That's a good question." I hesitated as I searched for another short answer. "Well. The father has sperm, and the mother has an egg. The sperm and egg get together in mommy's tummy and make a baby." The boys nodded, so I finished reading the story and then tucked them into bed.

A few days later, the boys wanted to read *Are You My Mother?* Again, the line "The egg jumped" sparked another question. Scott asked, "Mom, how did the egg and sperm get together?"

"Yeah," Ryan said. "How do they get into the mommy's tummy?"

"Do you get a shot?" Scott guessed.

"No, you don't get a shot, but those are great questions, guys." I didn't want to answer because they'd ask more questions, and it was bedtime, so I suggested, "How about we go to the library tomorrow and pick out some books about babies?" The boys nodded, and we returned to the story.

The next day, I picked the boys up at McNamara Elementary School and drove them to the library where they hopped out of the car, trotted toward the door, blond hair bouncing with each step. Once I entered the library, the boys had their hands on the counter and stood on their tip toes. "Excuse me," Ryan said.

The librarian leaned over, slid her glasses to the tip of her nose, and, with a smile, peered over the top. "Hi, boys," she said. "What can I help you with today?"

Ryan blurted, "Where are the books on how babies are made?"

She smiled and pointed. "In the back corner, along the bottom shelf."

"Thank you," Ryan and Scott said, then turned and began to sprint.

"Don't run, boys," I whispered, and their run slowed to a hurried skip. I was okay with the skip.

The boys pulled out several books and settled on three, which we read that evening. We sat on the floor cross-legged and learned about the parents' love, the penis, the vagina, the womb, and the inception.

Then Scott pointed to an illustration of sperm swimming toward the egg. "Look at this picture, Mom," he said. "There's a lot of sperm—and they look like tadpoles." He looked at me with a serious look. "Mom, if the sperm didn't get with the egg, would I be a frog today?"

I smiled and said, "No, you wouldn't be a frog. These sperm are for humans only."

For the next several months, the how-to-make-a-baby books had eliminated all questions until one evening when we read about a farmer who collected chicken eggs to sell at the market. Ryan interrupted, "Mom, about the eggs. You remember you said that only one egg and one sperm make a baby?" I nodded. "And there are millions of sperm. Can't more than one sperm get together with an egg?"

"No, only one sperm," I said.

"Even if it happens at the exact same time?" Scott interjected.

"One will always be first, even if it's a fraction of a second earlier." We sat on the floor, the boys more sedate than usual. This topic captured their attention.

"Mom, can women make babies all of their life?" Ryan asked.

"No, women can't, but men can," I answered.

"Why? That doesn't seem fair." Scott said. I grinned; I thought that was fair. A vision of me at seventy and pregnant flashed before me. I cringed.

My knees were stiff from sitting cross-legged, so I changed positions. "Well, women are born with a limited number of eggs," I replied.

"Do you still have eggs, Mom?" Scott asked. Questions flew at me, one after the other.

"Yes, I do."

"Good, then maybe I'll have a sister someday," Scott said. I responded that it could happen.

"How many eggs do women have?" Ryan asked.

"Each woman has a different amount, but only one egg a month is available," I said.

"What happens when you run out of eggs?" Scott inquired.

"It's called menopause, and it's a natural thing that happens when a woman can't have any more babies," I said.

"So, you'll be okay?" Scott looked at me with concern.

I ruffled his hair and said, "Yes, I'll be okay."

The following winter, the boys and I went to Pizza Hut. Mike, my husband, was out of town for work and would miss our little excursion. We ordered the usual, pepperoni pizza and Diet Coke. Sodas were not served at home, so this was a special treat. I passed out the plates, straws, and napkins the waitress left at the table while

Ryan and Scott discussed one of their Goosebumps books when, out of nowhere, Ryan leaped out of his seat and stood by the table. I wondered what he was doing, then, in a boisterous voice, he asked, "Mom, remember we read about a flower's stamens and pistils?" I nodded. "And how the pollen goes into the pistil to make a flower?"

"Yeah," I replied. I wondered where this line of questioning was leading, and Ryan had gained the attention of the diners around us.

"That made me think about humans and how the sperm gets to the egg," he said. I held my breath. The chatter in the room dulled, so his voice carried now. "Mom, tell me, exactly where is your vagina?"

What?

Dead silence. Scott knelt on his seat, elbows on the table, and leaned toward me; his blue eyes were wide with anticipation. Ryan stood there with his arms out to his side, head tilted and motionless, waiting for my reply. I glanced around the restaurant. The other patrons whispered to each other and watched us out of the corner of their eyes. I took a deep breath and looked at the boys.

"Well," I spoke slowly, not sure what to say. I hate being the center of attention. "You're asking a question..." I paused and glanced around again. People were still watching, and I could only hear the clanging of pans from the kitchen. I took a deep breath and continued, "...about a private part...in a public place. Can we talk about this when we get home?"

"Okay," Ryan said, and he sat down, and the boys returned to their Goosebumps discussion.

From the audience, I overheard a variety of responses.

"Good answer!"

"Awe, I wanted to hear what you would say!"

"Where did you find that answer?"

One woman stopped by our table and asked, "Can I send my kids over to your house for a sex education class?" We both chuckled.

Once we arrived home and removed our winter coats and boots, I said, "Boys, I can answer your question now."

They turned and looked at me.

"My vagina is between my legs." I waited for their reaction, another question, perhaps?

"Okay," they said in unison and bounded off to play a game. I laughed. I half expected they'd ask exactly where my vagina was.

The following year, Ryan and Scott were upside down on the couch, their backs arched over the edge of the seat, heads toward the floor, and feet over the back of the couch—a position not uncommon for them. I sat on the adjacent loveseat and read aloud from a book, *Animorphs #32: Separation*, a story involving twins.

"Mom, how do you get twins if there's only one egg and one sperm?" Scott asked. "Yeah, that makes one baby. How do you get two?" Ryan added.

"There are two ways to get twins," I replied. "First, there could be one egg and one sperm that combine, and then it splits into two."

"Oh!" That got their attention. They slid off the couch and sat on the floor facing me.

"They are called identical twins," I added, "and because it's the same egg and sperm, the babies look alike."

"There are twins in my class, and they don't look alike," Scott said.

"That's right; not all twins look alike. And that is the other way twins are made." They leaned forward with their eyebrows raised. I could tell they were trying to figure out how that worked.

"There are two eggs instead of one." I paused, watching for any reactions.

"But mothers only have one egg a month," Ryan said.

"Right, but a woman's body can release two eggs by mistake. It doesn't happen very often."

"Two eggs and two sperm," Scott said, half question and half statement.

"Yup, each egg will combine with a different sperm, but the babies aren't identical. They are called fraternal twins," I said. "It could be two boys, two girls, or even a boy and a girl. They're just like any other brother or sister."

"When the babies are born, how do they know if the twins are identical or fraternal?" Scott asked. I paused, amazed at the questions they asked.

"The doctor will tell the parents. If the egg and sperm split into two, the twins will be in one sac."

"So, if there are two eggs and two sperm, then there are two sacs?" Ryan asked.

"Yup. Identical twins have one sac; fraternal will have two."

Later that summer, Ryan played with his Legos while Scott and I rollerbladed along one of the community's paved pathways. I was a novice, and Scott, at eight years of age, was the teacher. He was in front of me and skated backward, watching me. "You're doing great, Mom, but keep your arms down. You don't want to look like a beginner."

"Okay," I said and lowered my arms, still a little unsteady and moving at a snail's pace. Then I saw Sue, a young mom who lived nearby. She pushed a double stroller.

I mentally reviewed the instructions Scott taught me. Put your foot forward, place the rubber stopper on the heel of the rollerblade on the ground, and apply pressure. I slowed to a stop in front of her.

"Hi, Sue," I said. "How are you and the girls doing?" I leaned over the stroller to get a closer look. They were smiling, arms waving in the air, and they wore matching pink shorts and a white top imprinted with a purple daisy. "They are adorable, and I see they have your smile."

"Thanks, they're beginning to crawl, so that keeps us busy," she replied.

Scott, who had been rollerblading in circles around us flipping between forward and backward, stopped next to the stroller. He leaned over, looked at the girls, then looked up at Sue and said, "Excuse me. Can I ask a question?" She smiled and nodded.

"Are they twins?" Scott asked.

"Yes, they are."

He paused, then asked, "One egg or two?"

28

THE SWEETEST GLASS OF WATER

JOHN VALLIATTU & DINESH J. JOHN

The year was 1980. I was a young heart surgeon who had just moved from India to a small Middle Eastern country with only one hospital for heart surgery. I had returned home to India (with my psychiatrist wife) after training in England but had to make the difficult decision to move to greener pastures. The chief surgeon was a local man who had trained in England at about the same time as I did. He was a nice man, but wouldn't let me operate. I would be his assistant for the time being. Professional jealousy can affect even good people.

Summer came. The scorching heat of the Middle East coupled with the winds (known locally as Shamal) created oppressive, even dangerous conditions. My chief went on vacation with his family to Europe. He ordered the central air conditioning of the operating rooms to be replaced during his absence. He also sent the heart-lung perfusionists, who are vital team members, on leave. The perfusionists' job was to run the heart-lung machine which kept the patient alive while the surgeon performed open heart surgery. So, for me that summer—no operating room (OR), no A/C, no perfusionist. And no possibility of heart surgery in the country. Or so I thought.

To be fair, the hospital was older, and the A/C units probably could have done with replacement. The trouble was that if there was a cardiac emergency, sick patients would have to be flown to another country to get the care they needed. And not all those patients would have been in a condition to survive the journey. I would, of course, travel with such critically ill patients to stabilize them to the best extent possible.

I still went to the hospital, where I saw patients in my clinic. That summer had record temperatures. Hot enough to melt my stethoscope in my car. One afternoon, I saw a local man in his long, flowing robes pushing a wheelchair down the corridor with a woman slumped in it. The patient was coughing out blood and collapsed right in front of me. I rushed her to the intensive care unit, introduced a breathing tube, and connected her to a ventilator. Blood and froth welled up in the breathing tube. I took a quick history and physical. The husband told me that his wife had had a heart valve replacement a few years before. I listened to her heart with my stethoscope. I heard a ringing sound for a few seconds, and then the ringing suddenly stopped.

That was trouble. The mechanical metallic valve was not working. We did an X-ray. The valve was missing from the heart and was lodged in the abdomen where the aorta, the main channel that carries fresh blood to the body, bifurcated. Without a valve to direct the flow forward, blood was backing up into her lungs. Time was not on her side, with the air-filled lungs turning solid with every passing minute.

This young lady was dying. She needed urgent surgery. It was life or death, for her, and me. I was young and foolhardy. If I dared to operate when my boss was away and things went wrong, which was more than likely in this scenario, it could spell an early end to my career as a cardiac surgeon. A young and impetuous inner voice said "You can't let her die without trying. You have to operate." That came out loud and clear.

That word was the trigger. A call for action if I ever heard one. The nurses ejected the workers from the operating room that was being renovated and threw out as much debris as they could. But I harbored no illusions that the operating room was clean or sterile. The anesthesiologists, whose job was to put the patient to sleep during surgery, agreed to take the risk. The husband of the young lady also understood the gravity of the situation and signed the high-risk consent form. But a crucial question still stared me in the face.

Who would run the heart-lung machine? My friend and colleague Dr. Pillai, offered to run this critically important piece of equipment. He had observed perfusionists running these machines during his training and had put together perfusion circuits. Dr. Pillai was fairly confident that he could do the job. But then, we caught a break. Word got around the hospital about the sick young lady, and a young physician approached me, "My sister is a first-year student in perfusion technology in Glasgow and she is at home for the summer." I told him, "Call her immediately."

Then he came back running. "A family friend who is a senior perfusionist in Canada is on vacation here. Should I call him?" This was too good to be true. "Please ask him to come," I replied. Then I got a phone call from the Canadian perfusionist, "Doctor, I am not licensed to work in this country." I said, "Don't waste time on trivial things. I will take full responsibility." Then a sheepish voice came over the phone, "Doctor, I am not a human perfusionist. I work in the animal lab."

I had a solution, "Just imagine this is a large dog," I told the perfusionist.

So, the motley crew was assembled. The unconscious lady, with only a wisp of life, was wheeled into the operating room. It was like a sauna. The anesthesiologist took a break every five minutes to change his sweat-soaked scrubs. But I did not have that luxury. After five hours of blood, sweat, and emotional turmoil, the surgeon who hadn't operated for a year, the animal perfusionist who had never worked on humans, and the brave souls who volunteered for this dangerous mission had fixed a new valve into the heart. Blood was pumped back in. The heart slowly blushed and came back to life. The new valve played new rhythms. But by then I was drenched, dehydrated, and fit to drop. A kind nurse brought a glass of water with a makeshift plastic straw fashioned out of an intravenous tubing set, pulled down my mask, and raised it to my lips. That was the sweetest glass of water I ever drank.

One more decision needed to be made: should we open the patient's abdomen and attempt to take the displaced valve out from the aorta? The valve that caused all this trouble in the first place. We looked around us at the carnage from the previous five hours of surgery, the filthy operating room, and the exhausted souls within, and decided enough was enough. Reassuringly, the anesthesiologist could feel the pulses in the patient's legs indicating that the runaway valve was not obstructing blood flow. The second surgery would have to wait for another day. In any case, our patient would be put on blood thinners for a while. This also would ensure that the old, displaced valve would not cause clotting at the site, and bought us time to plan this surgery in more ideal circumstances.

Miracle of miracles, my young patient did not have any postoperative infection. We gave her high doses of antibiotics to reduce the risk. Still, there was always a high possibility that the dirty operating room conditions would undo our hard work. By the grace of God, my young patient pulled through without further events.

I subsequently found out that this type of valve complication had been reported twice before in the surgical literature. The surgeries were done in ideal circumstances: a functioning operating room, trained perfusionists, and air-conditioning (I'd imagine). And sadly, in both cases, the patients succumbed to the complication.

That fateful day was a turning point in my career. My reputation as a skillful and responsible cardiac surgeon grew overnight among my colleagues, coworkers, and beyond. Even the nation's Minister of Health came to hear about this young lady's successful surgery against all odds. I was worried about my boss's possible reaction. Except for the fact that he did not speak to me for three days on his return, he quickly returned to his normal self, and we had a great partnership for many years thereafter.

Ten days after her surgery, the lady of my story walked out hand in hand with her man: a far picture from the day she came in. Never before and never after has cardiac surgery been done in such improbable circumstances. I became a heart surgeon that day. [1]

---

1. This piece was written by Dinesh John based on the interview he had with his father, John Valliattu.

About the Editors

Apple An is a professor at Syracuse University with 200+ publications, three books, and 15,500+ citations. She was her field's first historian, and founding editor-in-chief of a research journal, and was recognized with multiple awards for research, teaching, and service. Apple grew up during China's Cultural Revolution and came to the U.S. in her 20s. Apple writes about her life and those of people she knows. Her goal is to enrich Asian American cultural heritage and history and to enhance cultural understanding and acceptance among all people. Learn more at www.AppleAnBooks.com.

Georgia A. Popoff is a writer, editor, arts-in-education specialist, and program coordinator for the YMCA of Central NY's Writers Voice, where she teaches poetry and creative nonfiction. Her fourth collection of poetry, *Psychometry*, released in late 2019 by Tiger Bark Press, was a finalist for Utica College's Eugene Nassar Poetry Prize and the CNY Book Award for Poetry. Tiger Bark Press released her fifth collection, *Living with Haints* in spring 2024. In 2022, Georgia was named Poet Laureate of Onondaga County for a 2-year term of service. She is the series editor for the University of Michigan Press *Under Discussion* book series on contemporary poets. Visit www.georgiapopoff.com and follow her on Facebook, Instagram and Twitter: @gappoet.

About the Contributors

Jean Ann has a PhD in Linguistics and taught at SUNY Oswego for 25 years. She has been writing stories about her family of origin, among other things, since she could write. She supposes that if broken chifforobes can end up whole, maybe there's hope for the rest of us.

Leslie Ellen Archer is a writer retired from a career in theater design and production. She brought hundreds of stories to life on stage in collaboration with visual artists, musicians, dancers and her favorite collaborators, teenagers. She taught stage arts and creative writing in elementary, middle and high school classrooms, and in conjunction with arts projects at Syracuse University and Oswego State University. She is working on two soft science fiction series for young adult readers.

George Barber was born in Dundee, Scotland, in 1950. He worked in the restaurant business for 51 years and thus considers himself graduated from the College of Life, even though he officially graduated high school at age 39 in 1989. In 1977, he was married to a woman, but in 2015, he remarried to a man and is now happily living in New York City.

Holly Besaw is a lay servant, pet-therapy volunteer, and retired educator who lives in rural Upstate New York. She is the author of a rare-disease poem and two books for the children she visits with her therapy cats. Deeply religious, Besaw draws strength and inspiration from her faith.

Ann Sutera Botash, MD, a pediatrician and writer, serves as a SUNY Distinguished Teaching Professor at Upstate's Golisano Children's Hospital, Syracuse, NY, and specializes in the treatment of child abuse. A graduate of Vassar College, she grew up in Poughkeepsie and has received multiple regional and national teaching and advocacy awards.

Harriet Brown is a professor of Magazine, News & Digital Journalism at Syracuse University. She's the author of eight nonfiction books, including, most recently, *Shadow Daughter: A Memoir of Estrangement*. Her work has been translated into half a dozen languages.

Susan Burgess writes fiction and creative nonfiction. She is currently working on a series of essays and a novel, *The Fairy Tale*. She lives in Seattle, Washington, where she is constantly amazed and inspired by the beauty of the Pacific Northwest.

Karen C. Chamis was born just north of Buffalo, New York, and spent the following years living in NYC, New Jersey, and the DC area. She's grateful to have landed in Syracuse, a place that has very quickly become home. Karen's worked most of her life as a pastor, but in the time and space outside of that calling she's been active in community theater, fiber arts, and writing of all sorts. She completed a PhD in Organizational Leadership in her late 50s and lived to tell the tale. She has one spouse, one adult child (who also has one spouse), and one cat. Publishing credits include a back page essay in *Interweave Knits*.

Gwenlyn Davis loathed the purpose behind working in advertising design, consumerism; both before and after graduating from Empire SUNY, so she's held many titles: life-skills instructor, activity leader, daycare teacher, stage manager, bartender, and photographer, before finding passion for writing a memoir. "Thought I Knew Something About Breast Cancer," appears in the anthology, *Hopeful, Grateful, Strong*. Her memoir is yet untitled.

Carol Decker lives in Fayetteville, NY. She attended OCC, Syracuse University, and LeMoyne College, where her poetry was published in *The Salamander* in 2007. Her book, *Growing Up Invisible: A Young Girl's Odyssey*, a biographical fiction is available on Amazon. She is close to finishing her second book, *Thrust into Motherhood: A Young Woman's Odyssey*, which takes the reader through her adventures in high school, the shock of pregnancy, marriage, growing into motherhood, her mistakes, and her need to be loved.

Shannon Farrell is a scientist, non-fiction writer, and mother of two living in Syracuse, NY. With an undergraduate degree from Brown, a PhD from Texas A&M, and a stint as a college professor under her belt, she spends her free time hiking with her sons and writing her blog at motherhoodmultitudes.com.

Mary C. Gillen graduated with a BA from CUNY Queens College, Flushing, NY. She dreamed of writing mystery stories since age 8. She dreamed and delayed. Now, at the tender age of 83, she has returned to the Writers Voice Program, joined two professional mystery/crime writers organizations: Sisters in Crime and Queer Crime Writers. Moving Forward!

Sandy Greenberg spent their childhood, adolescence, and young adulthood in Rhode Island. After studying linguistics at Brown University, they worked in the nonprofit sector and as a collegiate debate coach. They currently live in Syracuse, New York, working in human services. Sandy writes about whatever catches their interest; the resulting hodgepodge could charitably be described as "eclectic."

Samuel D. Gruber is an architectural and urban historian, historic preservationist, and community activist. He is the author of books, chapters, reports, articles, and blogs about Jewish and medieval art, architecture, and historic sites. Sam has lived in Syracuse's Westcott neighborhood, about which he is writing a book, since 1994.

Felicia Haury graduated from the University of California, Berkeley. She was born and raised in Southern California and has worked as a Professional Fiduciary and Social Worker. She completed the Pocket MFA Non-fiction cohort in Winter 2023. Her poem, "Crab as a metaphor for don't f*** with me," was published in 12/2023 Lighthouse Anthology, *All the Lives We Ever Lived*. She is an avid antique shopper and experiments writing poetry, fiction, and non-fiction with equal enthusiasm.

Karen Foresti Hempson, an Upstate New York resident, is a retired professor of Social Studies Education. Her self-published book, *Bean Pickers, American Immigrant Portraits*, won first place for memoir in the NLAPW (National League of American Pen Women) Biennial Writing Competition. Excerpts were awarded by William Faulkner-William Wisdom Writing Competition as finalists. She recently completed a YA coming-of-age historical fiction, *Shellback*.

Tracy Chamberlain Higginbotham inspires women to support women in business, sports, equality, and life issues. She is a twenty-year blogger, past newspaper columnist, and author of "Under the Rose-Colored Hat," a story about living with alopecia. She is also dedicated to trying every sport once in her lifetime. To learn more, visit www.TracyHigginbotham.com.

Amy James was raised in Clinton, NY, on a steady diet of musical theater albums, her Welsh Nana's stories and songs, and books of all sorts. After graduating from Colgate University with a major in Theater and English, she worked variously as a singing clown, a window dresser, a coat check girl, a small-town newspaper writer, and a sometime actor and singer. A lover of words, she writes to process, document, and entertain (mostly herself).

Dinesh J. John is a physician executive who lives in Jamesville, NY. He works for Molina Healthcare, a Fortune 500 company, and previously worked as Chief Quality Officer at SUNY-Upstate Healthcare System in Syracuse, NY.

Sarah Mawhorter is a writer, urban scholar, teacher, and gardener living in Leiden, South Holland, where she can often be found walking or cycling along the canals with her husband and dog. A Southern California native, she has lived in Texas, Michigan, Scotland, Germany, Minnesota, and Central New York.

Marissa Montgomery is an academic writer, who lives in Central New York. This is her first autobiographical piece. Her years researching the historical and cultural roots of systemic misogyny finally provoked her to write about her own life experiences. This piece is part of a larger memoir that demonstrates the power of dreamwork to intervene and interrupt repetitive cycles of violence.

Mary Nowyj is a lifelong resident of Syracuse. She graduated from Syracuse University with a Master's degree in Communication Studies. She has published with *Centering, Grief Digest*, and *Arcadia Publishing Images of America for the Town Of Onondaga*. Some of her personal interests include book clubs, sports, theater, travel, and volunteering for non-profit organizations.

Sylvia O'Connor, poet and writer, lives with her husband Dennis in Syracuse, NY. Her writing quest began 20 years ago with a simple question: How can one say so much with so little? She is currently completing a memoir centered on the devastating impact of living decades with chronic Lyme disease and then recovery.

Kimberly Parr is a true crime writer who likes her cases cold and old. After a long career writing award-winning ad copy and feature articles for publications from *Equine Journal* to *Roofing Magazine*, she now writes exclusively about unsolved crimes at least 25 years old. A Maryland native, Kim lives in Manlius, NY, not far from the Erie Canal. Look for her on Medium, The Crime Wire, and IceColdCases.com.

Aaron M. Perrine is a lifelong upstate New Yorker who has settled in Syracuse with his wife and son. When he isn't working with highly regulated sentences, he can be found at local coffee-houses reading and crafting unregulated phrases, sentences, and paragraphs.

Lee B. Savidge, award-winning author and poet, retired military veteran, and corporate engineer, graduated from Rensselaer Polytechnic Institute and Syracuse University, active in Syracuse, New York, writing groups, is published in anthologies, *The Weight Of My Armor* (Parlor Press, 2017), and *What We See On Our Journeys* (Willet Press, 2021).

Jacqueline Schmitt graduated from LaFayette Central School and credits excellent English teachers for her love of a good book. After a career in public service, she now lives downstate and devotes her time to going to concerts, visiting museums, and writing about the people of New York State.

Jackie Southard and her husband, Mike, lived in upstate New York until they retired. They now reside in Greer, SC, and their two sons, Ryan, Scott, and Scott's wife Laura, live nearby. Jackie is writing a memoir about raising their inquisitive and curious sons, and this piece is part of her collection.

John Valliattu is an award-winning pediatric heart surgeon who has (literally) touched over 14,000 patients' hearts in a career spanning over 50 years. He is currently an administrator and surgeon at Believers Church Medical College Hospital in India.

DEAR READER

If you enjoyed this book, please leave a review to help other readers decide if this is a book they will enjoy.

If you would like to read more of Apple's literary journey, including news, updates, freebies, media coverages, etc., please sign up for her free newsletters at https://appleanbooks.substack.com/ or with the following QR code.

Apple An's Book Bytes
(AABB) Newsletters

Thank you!

From the multi-award-winning author

Apple An

Visit AppleAnBooks.com

Voices Heard Publishing, LLC

Daughter of Blue City

A Novel of Coming-of-Age Through Revolutionary China
© 2025

In the turmoil of China's Cultural Revolution, young Lianlian's life is shattered by family violence, public shame, and crushing poverty. Raised by a resilient but scarred mother, shadowed by an abusive father, and anchored by a little sister, Lianlian learns to survive a life with an impossible future. When the political climate shifts, she discovers that her mind is her only weapon and education is her only hope. Fueled by fierce determination and the quiet support of her mother, Lianlian battles for a spot at a top university, seeing it as her one true path to a life she can call her own.

If you like books about Chinese culture by **Amy Tan, Lisa See**, and **Pearl S. Buck**, and books about coming-of-age such as *A Tree Grows in Brooklyn* by **Betty Smith**, you will like this book!

"A deeply moving coming-of-age novel." – **Derrick Meade**

"Impossible to put down." – **TQ Pub**

"What touched me most was how her mother and sister gave her quiet strength." – **Sammy Moon**

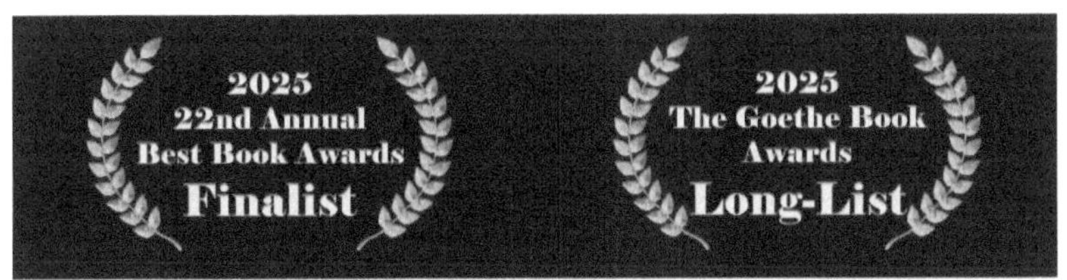

Mother of Red Mountains

A Novel of a Woman's Journey Through Revolutionary China
© 2024

An ambitious civil engineer desperately wants to protect her baby girls in the shadow of China's tumultuous mid-20th century. Despite tragedies in her childhood, Jun crafts a stable life by changing her name twice to fit in a male-dominated and politically charged society. Ambitious and high-achieving in her career, she seeks help from her in-laws to care for the girls. But the in-laws' capitalist class makes them all prime targets for the Red Guards at the onset of the Cultural Revolution in 1966. Jun worries about the well-being of her toddler girls, as they constantly witness their grandparents, and their own safety, being violated. Will Jun triumph over the grave danger she encounters and successfully protect and maintain a stable life for herself and her babies?

"Historical fiction/drama at its finest." - **Pikasho Deka**

"Lucid storytelling." - **Carmen Tenorio**

"I was transferred into this character and went through this journey with her." - **Harley Grace**

"The emotions feel universal and timeless." - **Hopper**

Las Crosses

An Unwavering Journey to a New Life in America © 2023

Fleeing the aftermath of the Tiananmen Square crackdown in 1989 and fueled by a burning desire for a better life, Apple embarks on a daring journey to pursue her doctoral education in America. With no backup plan, Apple must make this journey work. But she has no idea that her starting place, Las Cruces, NM, is a quiet desert town - a far cry from the bustling metropolis she envisioned. Anxious, ignorant, and homesick, Apple faces challenges she never had before. But she is determined to be open-minded. Excited and curious, will she simply survive the fish-out-of-the-water situation many immigrants experience, or will she thrive in this unexpected American adventure?

"A story of opportunity, bravery and self-invention that's as suspenseful and inspiring as it is quintessentially American." **- Jonathan Dee**

"Powerfully depicts scenes, characters, and emotions with bits of comedy." **- Cate McGowen**

"An enjoyable and essential read on cultural contrast from a historical era." **- Ginnah Howard**

"An inspiring story of resilience, hope and joyful curiosity, even in the face of uncertainty and difficulty. Uplifting!" **– Diane Pienta**

37 More Voices

Voices Heard Anthology Series, Vol. 2 © 2025

Beyond the everyday, what hidden wisdom awaits in the tapestry of our lives? Picking up where Volume 1, *28 Voices*, left off, this captivating second collection of essays invites you on a profound exploration of discovery and reflection.

Through a diverse array of personal narratives, these pages delve into the myriad ways we learn and grow. From the quiet revelations of self-awareness to the complex dynamics of family and friendship, discover the profound impact of connection. Uncover unexpected insights from the loyalty of pets, the discipline of hobbies, and the expansive perspectives gained from travel and exploration. Ultimately, these essays illuminate how every experience—large or small—contributes to the ever-evolving landscape of our personal philosophies and worldviews.

Join us on a journey of introspection that celebrates the richness of life's lessons, beautifully told.

All-in-One Dotted Journal Notebook

For a Busy, Productive & Mindful Life © 2023

Planners + Organizers + To-dos + Reminders + Trackers + Journals + Random Notes + Doodles + Nuggets of Goodness.

Do you have a busy life? Do you want to be productive? Do you want to have an efficient assistant to provide notes when you need it? Do you want to eliminate loose papers and memos? Do you want to have fewer notebooks or journals to deal with daily? Do you want to spend minimum time preparing your templates and more time to be productive and enjoy life? This All-in-One Dotted Journal Notebook might be just what you need.

Give this a try for one month. There is no need to waste money if it does not work for you. You can find examples to guide you to developing your own habits and uses.

"Takes getting organized to a new level!" - **Joseph Brennan**

"I absolutely love this planner! If you're looking for an efficient planner, this is worth considering." - **Angela Dorris**

"I appreciate most about this notebook is the upfront guidance and examples. It inspired me to use the notebook in ways I never would have thought of." - **Leon Edward**

"I am pleased with the large number of flexible templates for my various needs." - **Kateryna Hlushchenko**